X
and
WHY

X and WHY

The rules of attraction: why gender still matters

Tom Whipple

Published in 2018 by Short Books Ltd
Unit 316, ScreenWorks, 22 Highbury Grove,
London, N5 2ER

10 9 8 7 6 5 4 3 2 1

A CIP catalogue record for this book is available
from the British Library.

ISBN: 978-1-78072-348-8

Cover design by Evie Dunne
Printed at CPI Group (UK) Ltd, Croydon, CR0 4YY

To Catherine

For, among many things, attempting to explain to our nanny why the kitchen calendar had an entry reading "Sex Party!!!!"

CONTENTS

INTRODUCTION

Tell me more, tell me more, did you get very far? Tell me more, tell me more, like does he have a car?

Olivia Newton John and John Travolta

One spring day in 2009, Laerke Bjerager spotted a man she fancied, walked up to him on a busy Copenhagen shopping street and asked him for sex. He said yes.

Then she went and asked another, and another, and another.

She found the men didn't always say yes, at least not immediately. Sometimes, they were worried they might be part of a practical joke. Then, she had to convince them. "They were apprehensive, and curious," she says. Which seems reasonable; nothing in their life so far would have convinced them that this was a plausible scenario. Notwithstanding, most took a punt on it eventually and agreed to sleep with her.

Those that didn't generally had girlfriends. So they had to, regretfully, decline. "They were apologetic, they didn't want to hurt your feelings." It was, she says, a "very efficient confidence boost".

Elsewhere in Denmark, Kaare Bro Wellnitz was asking the same question but having the opposite experience. His confidence, in fact, was taking a bit of a bashing. By the end of his first day he had had "no real yeses". There was one woman who said yes, but she was laughing – and it was more a "yeah, sure" rather than a "yes, please".

At least this woman wasn't offended – or worse, scared – as many were when he asked them for sex. "One girl...was afraid if I was some kind of lunatic." He could see her point. He felt slightly mad too. "It was very hard to put yourself up to it. It was...very...very strange."

It wasn't so strange, though, that he wasn't sure what he would say if the roles were reversed, and he was asked for sex. "If a girl came up to me, I would be one of those guys who'd say, 'Yeah, sure. It's a nice opportunity.'"

If he had said yes then, like all the other men, a few seconds later he would have learnt the offer was a sham. Because no one ended up having sex. These Danish students were repeating an experiment on gender differences in casual sex that is not just a classic in the field, it is probably *the* classic in the field. In fact, it has even inspired a pop song.

ᐧ ᐧ ᐧ

A few years ago I covered a science festival for my newspaper, *The Times*. There was a talk about gender, and on the stage a panel of scientists and sociologists argued about whether the term even made sense. Could gender itself, they asked, be a social construct?

It's a fair question. Between bisexuals, homosexuals, trans-sexuals, pansexuals and asexuals, are we not just all on a spectrum? If a trans man can in theory have a genetically related baby through a surrogate mother, fertilised using artificial insemination from his male partner, what, in every sense of the word, is sex?

In a decade spent writing about science, I have seen and experienced the controversy about gender – the behaviour that attaches to our chromosomal sex – and what it means. I have seen scientists attacked for suggesting there are innate differences between male and female brains; I have seen scientists attacked for saying there aren't. I have seen male chess grandmasters claim that their game is a uniquely male pursuit; I have seen female chess grandmasters get rather cross with them.

I have covered stories in which professors on two sides of the gender debate were simultaneously sending me abusive emails about the other.

In that tent at that science festival, though, it was not the discussion that struck me as interesting, but the people watching it. Here was an audience of all ages happily listening to ideas that even in their lifetimes would have seemed ludicrous, but today are utterly uncontroversial.

It seemed everyone in the marquee was on board with the idea that pink toys for girls are pernicious. They were equally united in the belief that toy guns and swords for boys are restrictive, that girls are just as good at science, and that a lack of paternity leave harms men and children alike. More than this, many left that marquee apparently content in the idea that gender identity can be a choice – not a chromosome.

Then, on leaving the marquee, a large portion of them turned right. They walked along the path and came to another tent. And here they queued up for the toilet – perfectly happy with the idea that they happened to choose the one determined by their sex. In a very minor way, minutes after the talk, biological differences had already affected behavioural ones.

Sometimes change never seems to come. Sometimes it happens so fast that you only notice it afterwards.

Two years earlier I had myself gone on five months of paternity leave. I was the first in my office to take advantage of a new UK law that made this possible, and colleagues made jokes about how I would have to learn how to lactate. One friend helpfully suggested my baby would soon be able to suckle using the "disgraceful remnants of [my] fast-withering ball sack". But by the time I returned to work, two other new fathers had already made the decision to do the same – and their choice went unremarked upon.

Gender is shifting. But is gender disappearing? Are we really seeing a reassessment of not just the relations between men and women but the very idea of "men" and "women", at least beyond the physical facts of our birth? Is this the last, and greatest, battle of the sexual revolution of the 1960s?

Perhaps. If so, though, it is clear that this is still a work in progress – something society is cautiously, tentatively, trying to understand. There are unresolved contradictions. If, for instance, gender really is a social construct, if there is no such thing as a female and a male brain, then how can we also argue that gender is so important we should operate on people whose brain tells them they are a different sex?

Statistics tell us that 99 per cent of those present in the marquee that day – given there were fewer than 300 people there, quite possibly 100 per cent – were comfortable in their gender. Estimates of the proportion of people with "gender dysphoria" hover around 0.3 per cent.[1] That might change. We might find that our genders really are more fluid and switchable – that humans can escape the apparent shackles of biology. Or we might find, once everything settles, that gender fluidity is about a timely resettling of stereotypes, but that gender itself still remains, as strong as ever. Because if gender is a social construct, for now it feels remarkably well constructed. And, for most people, it still defines our lives in ways that no amount of social conditioning can explain.

Maybe as a girl you preferred to play with tractors, and climb trees with boys? Wonderful. But when you went through puberty, you still knew that if you had sex with one of those boys it was you who would get pregnant. A womb is not a patriarchal creation.

Or were you a boy who enjoyed pushing dolls around in prams and watching cartoons starring Disney princesses? There's nothing at all wrong with that. But as a teenager you would have still experienced a surge in testosterone and been aware that the basic act of reproduction involved the effort not of nine months but ten minutes.

The physical facts of the body cannot always be thought of as an inconvenient mask, irrelevant to our behaviour.

This is a book about the place where biology meets behaviour. It is about where sex differences in our bodies most closely (but not always) translate into gender differences in the choices we make and what we do. It is ultimately a call to remember that, amid the tumult of changing politics, gender matters. The biggest psychological difference between the sexes, after all, is one so ubiquitous many do not even notice it as a difference. That difference? Most women find men attractive; most men do not.

The reason why is the reason why sexes exist at all: sex, in the reproductive sense. This book is about the scientific investigations into how, and why, the two sexes approach sex differently. It will not look into many wider issues of gender, as they stretch beyond sex – that is for another book. But for those looking for answers as to why genders exist at all, sex is all you need. That does not mean, though, that the answers are simple.

For Jane Austen in the 18th century, it was clear that a single man in possession of a good fortune must be in want of a wife. For *Cosmopolitan* in the 21st century, it is clear that a single man in possession of a social media account must be the one who texts first. At least, that is the case according to their latest "Does he like you?" quiz – the consensus changes.

Despite its reputation for certainty, science is often just as fuzzy. There are rarely definitive answers, particularly when it comes to human behaviour. Sometimes science will tell you what you want to hear, sometimes it will tell you what you don't. Sometimes it will flat out contradict itself. But that is not a reason for nihilism.

Truths are there. Conclusions can be reached, but not through the easiest path. The approach needed is more like a sailing boat's when tacking into the wind – you gather evidence from one direction, then another, until slowly the real direction of travel becomes clear, even if the destination remains only just visible, indistinct on the horizon.

For all that the controversy in this area is furious, pinning down the actual sources of disagreement is hard. Find yourself a feminist professor in a gender studies department and she will still, when pressed, accept that humans are not blank slates – that evolved differences exist in our psychology.

Find yourself a free marketeering red-in-tooth-and-claw evolutionary psychologist and he will still, sometimes grudgingly, accept that sex differences can be exacerbated, or even created, by social circumstances – that not everything in our psychology is immutable. The academic dispute is in degree, rather than absolute, and the heat can be greater than the light.

This book is my attempt to find some light, to tack my way to the truth. But this book is not The Truth. It is, like science itself, a collection of partial truths. Some of the studies I cite are indisputably true, but the strength of conclusions drawn from them are disputed. Some of the studies I cite will eventually turn out to be false, but maybe the approach taken still tells you something about where science is going. My hope is that together they create something that might just give you insight into your own life. And that insight, for all that we snigger about sex, matters. Sex is the crucible of evolution.

Behavioural differences between sexes, if we look at popular culture at least, go far beyond which bathroom you choose. John Travolta's male friends sang, of his summer loving, "Tell me more, tell me more, did you get very far?" while Olivia Newton John's sang, "Tell me more, tell me more, like does he have a car?" Her female friends wanted to know if it was love at first sight; Travolta's male friends were more interested in whether she "put up a fight".

Mills and Boon's bestsellers, read almost exclusively by women, include *Naughty Nights in the Millionaire's Mansion* and *The Billionaire Boss's Secretary Bride*, but not *The Penniless Artist's Menopausal Lover*. Male pulp literature, on the other hand, does not have a romance section. It has grizzled tough guys like Jack Reacher pummelling baddies in a righteous cause and then, incidentally along the way, picking up a woman 20 years their junior.

Differences in the sexes could explain why, if the stereotypes are true, those women want rose petals scattered on satin sheets in candlelit rooms, while the tough guy – if he's honest – could just make do with a flat surface and a willing partner.

They would explain why, when the tough guy finally settles down to a life in suburbia, his pummelling days behind him, he and his new love will grow happily old together – but might well also make that familiar confession that, even on their golden wedding anniversary, they never felt they completely understood each other.

But how much are the stereotypes just that – stereotypes?

In this book I will take you through my investigation of differences in how the two sexes approach love and sex. I will explore the science behind them – what these differences are, what we understand about the causes of them and, just as importantly, what we don't understand. I will travel from a gay penguin colony in Germany to a bungalow orgy in the Home Counties.

This book will not be an argument about nature over nurture. I don't believe there is a time in our prehistory when the ideal forms of men and women were created – their ids and superegos unchanged and unchangeable until today. Extrapolating from how our Stone Age ancestors evolved cannot help you understand everything about humans. Neither, though, is it pointless.

If you are currently single, this book is about your place in the dating market – your successes, your failures and what they mean. If you are married, it is about why you chose the person you are with, why they chose you – and the circumstances in which either of you might put it all at risk and stray.

And if you are one of the many people whose sexuality comes with a prefix – homo, bi, or trans – this book might just give you an insight into the emerging science behind the way you live.

In any case, it will show that love and sex are not quite as simple as a Mills and Boon novel would have you believe.

Mills and Boon, for instance, might have a lord of the manor as the chiselled hero, but why does the tousled stable boy so often get a look-in in romantic romps too? Don Juan might be remembered as a Casanova while Moll Flanders is a Scarlet Woman – but in some countries the distinction is fading. Those countries? The ones with more female MPs. Those are also the countries where those MPs' female constituents are more likely to be sexually interested in the other female constituents.

Instead of being minor anomalies, this book will show these are windows into the deeper, and continuing, mysteries of human sexuality and gender.

This is a book about expectations and mismatches. It is about love, sex and the trade-off between the two. It is about how the two sexes differ – and reach compromise – in the most ancient of biological imperatives: producing a new generation. It will start, though, with the most simplistic stereotype of all: the predatory male.

What is the evidence that men want sex more, how strong is that evidence – and to what extent can this be explained as something innate to their gender, rather than due to the society that they grew up in?

It is time to return to the streets of Denmark.

1

PRIAPUS

The predatory male

I've noticed you around. I find you very attractive. Would you go to bed with me?

In 1998 Touch and Go, a British band, released the song for which they are now best remembered. It had a catchy saxophone riff, a surreal video involving fried eggs, and lyrics largely consisting of one repeated phrase: "I've noticed you around, I find you very attractive. Would you go to bed with me?"

It seems safe to say this is the only song to draw its lyrics from the methods section of a psychology paper. Because the first time that that phrase was used, or at least verifiably used, was on a campus in Florida, in the late 1970s – after an argument in a tutorial.

Russ Clark, a psychology professor, had been teaching a lesson. He was discussing the correct interpretation of a recently published paper, about the attractiveness of people in bars. An empirical validation of beer goggles, the research showed people got hotter over the course of an evening. Years later, he and his colleague Elaine Hatfield documented what happened next.

Professor Clark, they wrote, "dropped a bomb" into the conversation – making just the sort of antiquated statement unlikely to go down well in a liberal university at the height of the sexual revolution. "'A woman,' he said, 'good-looking or not, doesn't have to worry about timing in search of a man. Arrive at any time. All she has to do is point an inviting finger at any man, whisper, "Come on 'a my place," and she's made a conquest. Most women,' he said, 'can get any man to do anything they want. Men have it harder. They have to worry about strategy, timing, and tricks.'"

"Not surprisingly, the women in the class were incensed," he and Professor Hatfield wrote, 20 years later. "One woman sent a pencil flying in Russ's direction." He was losing control rapidly. As a man of science, though, he had a riposte. "'We don't have to fight. We don't have to upset one another. It's an empirical question. Let's design a field experiment to see who's right!'"[2]

And so his students went into the street, approached members of the opposite sex, and said, "I've noticed you around, I find you very attractive, would you go to bed with me?" Just as in Denmark decades later, and in every one of the many experiments since that has repeated Hatfield and Clark's, the majority of men said yes – and 100 per cent of women said no.[3]

⌣‿⌣

The rocker Bill Wyman used to find the Australian weather a great assistance: it meant the girls could wait outside all night.

During his tour of the southern hemisphere with the Rolling Stones, the bassist developed a system. "Me and Brian used to look out of the windows, 'cos we shared a suite, and we would ask the night porter to go out and get the one in the striped thing and the one in the shorts next to her, and they'd come up, and you'd spend a couple of hours with them and say bye and give 'em a kiss, and then about half an hour later you'd say, 'That one in the red dress'."

One Direction, at least according to news reports, alighted on a similar method – updated for new technologies. A woman called Anna, 19, told press in 2015 that she had been part of their process for populating parties – after being approached by a security guard while at a club, again in Australia.

"He was very blunt. He wanted 20 girls and pictures sending straight away. It turns out they keep lists of girls from different places around the world – not with their real names though. They use nicknames to describe them. There were four of us in the end who went to the band's house outside Melbourne. The security team arranged to pick us up from a hotel, and sent a blacked-out car to fetch us."

It is not recorded what happened when they arrived – not least because the security guards also took their phones away from them.

Once upon a time, the men who had access to the most women were those who had slain their menfolk in battle. Now, by a strange quirk of civilisation, it is those who can play a guitar or act who can get any women they want. And this is precisely what they do, even if, today, it is something they want to keep secret. From Julio Iglesias with his reputed 3,000 lovers to Jack Nicholson with 2,000 ("Every age," he said. "Their mothers...some of them with their mothers."), male stars can amass heroic tallies of sexual conquest.

What about female stars? Some can certainly live the rock-and-roll lifestyle – Robbie Williams memorably said he was privileged to have "been in Take That and four out of five of the Spice Girls" – but the equivalent levels of legendary loving just does not seem to exist.

When a woman is universally desired, she seems to go for quality not quantity. Helen had a face to launch a thousand ships, but she had no intention of pleasuring each captain when he arrived. Marilyn Monroe was the pin-up of her generation, but she chose the playwright Arthur Miller to be the love of her life – reputedly flirting with the idea of Albert Einstein as an alternative.

More attractive men, studies have found, have more sexual partners. More attractive women do not.[4]

Of course, if Monroe had decided to exploit her position in the manner of Bill Wyman, she would have rapidly lost that position as an object of desire. Society, certainly at the time, would have viewed her in the same way as it views the only women who do approach Wyman's lifetime tally: as a prostitute. Men who have lots of sexual partners are at the top of society; women who do so are usually at the bottom.

So just because Monroe did not have nightly foursomes does not necessarily mean that she did not want to – she may not have been prepared to deal with the consequences. When she looked at the line-up of autograph hunters outside her dressing room, was she ever tempted to ask the security guard to pick two out, bring them inside, and then replace them with another pair a few hours later?

Answering that question – the question of why humans do things – is a lot harder than finding out what they do. And getting at the truth requires a lot more than just watching what happens when students proposition people in the streets.*

There are few more persistent stereotypes than the sexually rapacious male and the choosy female. It is a dynamic that can be seen in every nightclub in the western world, as confident men approach women to try their luck, while less confident men shuffle over and dance around them hoping against hope (and all prior experience) to win them over.

In more modest cultures the dynamic is still there. Outside the west, it is not the promise of a love match with a good woman that is used to motivate Islam's male suicide bombers: it is 72 demure virgins. For the rare female Jihadi, the Quran makes no such offer — but it seems unlikely that the prospect of 72 adolescent males pawing inexpertly at them in the afterlife would increase their motivation to blow themselves up.

Darwin put it thus in *The Descent of Man*, "The female... with the rarest exceptions, is less eager than the male...she generally 'requires to be courted'; she is coy, and may often be seen endeavouring for a long time to escape from the male. Every observer of the habits of animals will be able to call to mind instances of this kind."

Of course, Darwin noted, eventually the female relents — or none of us would be here. "It is shewn by various facts...

---

* There have been several studies that have investigated whether the sex difference found in the would-you-go-to-bed-with-me studies really is so great. The least convincing involved asking women if they would like casual sex with random strangers if they were Hollywood A-listers (they would). The most convincing is in a later chapter.

that the female, though comparatively passive, generally exerts some choice and accepts one male in preference to others. Or she may accept, as appearances would sometimes lead us to believe, not the male which is the most attractive to her, but the one which is the least distasteful."*

But was he right on this one aspect, the coyness of females and the eagerness of males?

A single study in a single place does not prove a truth about human psychology. Neither do the observations of one biologist – albeit the greatest one in history. Societies can change, and societies can surprise. Even Darwin's statement contains a controversy many would miss today – it ascribes power to the woman to choose, in a way that few would have acknowledged back then.

Ultimately we can never completely know what is going on in someone's head – in their drive for sex the two genders must always remain a mystery to each other. But by taking competing lines of evidence, across cultures, times and behaviour, we can begin to build up a more coherent picture – and arrive at the likeliest assessment of human sexuality.

Scientists have asked people about their attitudes to

---

* If you think this implies that Darwin might not have been the most romantic of chaps, it is interesting to note that before marrying he drew up a list of the pros and cons of entering into a union. His pros included "a nice soft wife on a sofa with good fire", "Constant companion, (and friend in old age) who will feel interested in one,— object to be beloved & played with— better than a dog anyhow", "Charms of music & female chit-chat". The cons, even more pragmatic, considered the potentially catastrophic effect on his social life. "Terrible loss of time," he wrote, as well as, "[Loss of] conversation of clever men at clubs...forced to visit relatives, and to bend in every trifle", and the alarming, "Perhaps my wife won't like London; then the sentence is banishment & degradation into indolent, idle fool."

casual sex in countries across the world. From America to Zimbabwe, the result is the same: men want more of it.[5] They have peered inside marriages. At every age, at every stage, husbands want more sex than their wives.[6] They have asked people their ideal number of lifetime sexual partners: among undergraduates, women said they wanted a bit over 1 and men on average wanted 14. Among those over 30 women still said they wanted a bit over 1, but men, seeing mortality on the horizon, upped their tally to 74 (a number heavily skewed by the occasional aspiring Wyman who wanted 1,000).[7]

They have looked at what happens when you remove women from the equation. Among gay men, acting without the brake of female caution, the prospect of achieving Wyman levels of partners suddenly becomes a reasonable aspiration for even non-rock stars. One pre-HIV survey in the US in 1978 claimed to have found that almost half of those quizzed had managed 500 sexual partners in their lifetime.[8] The scientist involved noted, "The subculture of gay men did briefly establish bathhouses and other institutions that allowed men to have sex with half a dozen or more partners in a single evening." Roy Baumeister, a US psychologist, lamented in his 2001 review of promiscuity, "Lesbian communities do not seem to have created any market for such institutionalized orgiastic behavior."[9]

What if you look at sexual acts that don't need a partner at all? The same picture emerges here too. Every study conducted has found that men masturbate more frequently, start doing so earlier in life – and maintain a hobbyist's interest in onanism well into old age. Two thirds of men say they would use a sex robot, while two thirds of women said they would not.[10] When people have casual sex, women are more likely to hope it becomes something romantic; men are more likely to hope it stays as just sex.[11] Priests, one brave researcher found, are more likely to break their vow of celibacy than nuns.[12]

The more people study it, the harder it is to argue that men and women have the same desire for sex. The consequences of this research go far further than the bedroom, though. Because this is not just about how men behave with women when sex is clearly on the agenda. It is about what happens in the office, the shops and the street. It is about every other interaction they have with women in the rest of their lives as well. It is about the language, signals, conversation and mannerisms of men and women who, even subconsciously, are aware that whenever they meet, they are meeting a potential sexual partner. Whether the feeling is mutual or not.

Amy Kinyon had had enough. The Safeway employee was sick of the looks, the menacing atmosphere, the intimidating customers. Most of all, she was sick of smiling. So much so that she joined with four of her colleagues to file a suit at the US Equal Employment Opportunity Commission – claiming that the company had created a "hostile work environment".

Their issue? A new "Superior Customer Service" policy, rigidly enforced by undercover shoppers, in which employees had to address customers by name, ask them about their day, make eye contact and – most of all – smile.

"The Company is forcing us to suspend our natural self-defense mechanism of avoiding contact with men who act inappropriately towards us," said Kinyon. Employees had reported that they were being harassed, touched, followed to their cars and propositioned. "I enjoy serving all of my customers, including our male customers," said Kinyon.

"And, almost all my male customers are no different from women shoppers. But there also are plenty of creeps out there or just plain lonely guys who 'hit on' us and we're open targets in these stores. The problem has always been there, but the new 'always-smile, always-make-eye-contact' rules have made it much worse."

Although the problem was vastly different in scale, this new policy was not just disliked by the employees. One of the male customers discombobulated by the policy was Norman Li, who happens to also be a psychologist. For him, when he learnt what was going on, it illustrated a fundamental truth about male and female interactions.

He wrote about it in a scientific article,[13] co-authored with colleagues (referring to himself somewhat tortuously as "First Author", to keep in scientific house style). "When the first author was in graduate school he often shopped for groceries in a Safeway store in Tempe, Arizona. Upon going through the checkout lane one day he was greeted by an attractive female clerk who smiled, made clear eye contact, and greeted him very warmly. Naturally [he] perked up and started a conversation with the young woman. She responded favourably, continuing to maintain eye contact and a beaming smile." The clincher, for the amorous Li, came when, having noted his details from his credit card, she "called out his name before having to tear herself away to attend to the next (less interesting of course) person in line." The next time he went to the shop he decided to step things up a notch – moving the conversation beyond small talk. He then became baffled when she seemed to resist. There was, he said, "some implicit resistance that seemed to contradict the flirtatious behaviour."

Li's experiences were an extreme example of something that happens everyday – that does, in fact, seem to be a crucial part of being a man. Namely, an inflated sense of one's own attractiveness.

In study after study, scientists have shown that men consistently overrate their own romantic appeal. If you ask speed daters after each interaction to assess how much the other person liked them, the men will always err on the optimistic side. This can lead to disappointment, for men, but also annoyance – or worse – for women.

It is why a gangly youth can spend the evening on a dancefloor pursuing a woman manifestly out of his league, believing he has a chance, simply because she is too polite to tell him to leave her alone. It is why stalkers can maintain fantasies of winning over women who despise them – and one reason why attractive women can sometimes find just a walk along a street to be a gauntlet of creepy men trying their luck.

But none of this means it is a bad thing for men to deceive themselves this way, from an evolutionary perspective. Quite apart from the fact that few teenage boys could make it through the sexual desert of adolescence without a whole suite of psychological buffers, there are good reasons why men should believe their probability of success to be higher than it is – and remain undaunted in the face of the obvious evidence they are wrong.

Li believes it is because, put simply, they have so little to lose by failing, and so much to gain by winning. If a man successfully judges a situation correctly, and has sex, he is able to make a baby and win in the genetic game of life. If he judges it incorrectly, he looks an idiot – a minor trade-off, compared to fulfilling the entire biological purpose of his existence.

In a twist on innocent until proven guilty, men seem to work on the basis that they are attractive until proved otherwise, and so take even the faintest encouragement as a full-on come-on.

For a woman, the calculus is very different. Given the results from the "Would you go to bed with me" study, judging whether a man wants her is not an especially difficult calculation. The second consideration is far more difficult. She also has to judge whether he will stick around afterwards to help her raise a baby – or at the very least whether his genetic stock is high enough that it is worth her investing a significant proportion of her life in raising his child to adulthood.

This is an intuitive version of a theory that has for the past half-century loomed large in every discussion of sex differences. It is Robert Trivers' Parental Investment Theory. In 1972, Trivers in effect formalised sexual politics by arguing that at its root, in every species, is the disparity in contribution to child rearing and gestation.

When one sex has to spend more time and energy on its offspring – for instance by gestating it – that sex would do better by being more choosy regarding who it mates with. Mating indiscriminately would risk putting a lot of effort into allying with bad genes, and with a feckless partner who would offer little in the way of help.

Conversely, if the other sex has to invest little – for instance a plausible smile and a nice glass of Sauvignon – it is incentivised to mate whenever it can. It's always a reproductive advantage to have more offspring, when having more offspring costs you nothing. This does not mean men never want to commit; a child brought up with the help of a father has a far greater chance of success. But it does mean that the calculus for them is very different.

When women are shown pictures of men with descriptions of their character, how attractive they rate them is affected by whether they are good or bad, reliable or unreliable. With men, the same pretty woman could be a human rights defender with an NGO or a cold-blooded terrorist: their attractiveness rating of her barely flutters.[14]

The power of this idea becomes clear in the exceptions. For instance, consider seahorses. The act of mating in seahorses is a transaction that involves the female literally transferring her eggs to the male, for him to look after and hatch. In most species females, the higher-investing sex, are choosier. Males compete to impress them, and copulate when they can.

But the seahorse is different. Here, the male provides the most obligatory investment to the offspring, carrying the eggs until they hatch – expending resources protecting and nurturing them while the female returns to her life. And with it, all the other roles are reversed too. The females are the larger sex, competing among themselves for male attention. The females woo, the males choose.[15]

~ _ ~

The opposite of opportunities seized, of *diems carped*, is regrets. In 1983 Sir John Betjeman was interviewed by the BBC for a retrospective of his life. A respectful interview was carried out along the windy Cornish coast, near the home he would soon die in. Here, as the blustery sea beat against a rugged beach, the presenter asked the septuagenarian poet whether, as he came to the end of his life, he had any regrets.

He thought about the question. "Yes," he said. "Yes. I haven't had enough sex."

Betjeman is far from alone in this sentiment. When asked to look back on their lives men, whether heterosexual or homosexual, consistently lament the times they didn't have sex but could have done so, while women, lesbians included, consistently lament the times they did.[16] And when those first American students went onto the street, and propositioned people for sex, they could already see those regrets – or lack of them – beginning to form in the responses of those who said no.

When Hatfield and Clark conducted their experiment, they recorded the manner of the rejections. "In general, the female experimenters reported that men were at ease with the request. They would say, 'Why do we have to wait until tonight?' or 'I cannot tonight, but tomorrow would be fine.' The men that said 'No' even gave apologies, ie, 'I'm married'... In contrast, the women's response to the intimate requests from males was 'You've got to be kidding,' or 'What is wrong with you? Leave me alone.'"

In Denmark, they found something similar. "The men were pleased. They said, 'That's funny, that really made my day'. They got high on it in a flattering way," said Henrik Høgh-Olesen, the University of Aarhus professor behind the study. As before, those who had to refuse offered excuses. "They said, 'I have a girlfriend coming to stay, could it be next week?' They apologised, they felt they had to – to excuse that they were not man enough to take this great invitation from a moderately attractive person."

Sometimes, said Professor Høgh-Olesen, the women

reacted in a manner that could almost come from a biology textbook. "They said, 'Aren't you able to make an effort? We need more effort.' They were saying, this is your job in this game – to make an effort and bring presents and gifts to convince me, while I have to be a bit reluctant in order to find a suitable partner."

A few days after the professor's experiment ended there was a knock on his door, from one of the men who had been propositioned. "He was a law student," says the professor. "When he found out that he was cheated he felt very stupid." More than that though, being a law student he wanted to establish his rights. Was this breach of contract? Was he owed a night of passion?

"He was very offended, he had found himself in a ridiculous situation where he had showed a part of himself he didn't want everybody to know about." After some diplomatic discussion, Professor Høgh-Olesen managed to salve his ego. "I made him calm down and, in the name of science, to take this defeat as a man."

⁓

Sex does not just make people ridiculous. It also sometimes makes them dishonest – whether consciously or unconsciously.

"Everywhere we look," proclaimed a 2013 article in *Cosmopolitan*, "there's sex winking right back at us." The author then, over the course of a brief paragraph, provided various sources of evidence for this sexual winking. TV, for instance. Music videos.

But, she lamented, there was a paradox. "With so much sexy time going on around us, surely we're having more bedroom action than ever, right? Wrong. Oh so wrong."

Alas, *Cosmo*'s crack team of sexperts had discovered that we were having marginally less sex than we used to. This was particularly surprising, they noted, because we had more sexual partners.

"Women now have an average of 7.7 sexual partners in their lifetime compared with just 3.7 recorded in 1991. And men now have an average of 11.7 partners whereas it was 8.6 in 1991."

What *Cosmo* had also stumbled upon was one of the absolute laws of sex statistics: that men have more partners than women.

The gap between the mean number of sexual partners for heterosexual men and women is a statistic that has been confirmed more often than Clark and Hatfield's "Would you go to bed with me" study. The numbers may change, but the existence of the gap does not – across time and across cultures. Neither does the press's interest in it.

According to a news story in the *Sun*, in 2014, men have 12 partners, while women have eight. The *Scottish Sun* in 2007 found similar figures, and it also had better data and was able to break down both activity and number by region. (This enabled it to note, for instance, "RANDY and adventurous Highlanders are most likely to make the most of our beautiful countryside and head outside for sex. A whopping 80 per cent of horny and hardy Highlanders claimed they were most likely to strip off and get back to nature by getting dirty making love outdoors.")

The disparity has been noted in every men's and women's magazine with a sex column, and in many without, and is found in every sex survey conducted since sex surveys began.

There are variations of it. For instance, according to the *Guardian* the disparity spreads to individual dates: one in ten men and one in 30 women had sex on a first date with their current partner.

Even the *Wall Street Journal* accepts it as reality. In an advice column it tackled the question. "In a New Relationship, Should You Reveal How Many People You've Slept With?" It noted, sagely, "Most people don't want to know the number; studies say men typically have more partners."

So it seems Darwin, and the cultural stereotype he believed, is correct. It is indeed "shewn by various facts" that the female is "less eager than the male". Or, as his contemporary William Acton – Victorian doctor and, as *Cosmo* would say, sexpert – famously put it, "the majority of women (happily for society) are not very much troubled with sexual feeling of any kind."

There are few better validated statistics: throughout history and throughout the world, men have more sexual partners. There's just one problem with that result. It's mathematically impossible.

Yes, men are as eager as the stereotypes suggest. But women, it turns out, are nowhere near as coy – even if they pretend otherwise.

2

APHRODITE

Woman and suppressed sexuality

I was an absolute trollop when I was a Land Girl. No, I wasn't sleeping the night with them – it was more roadside sex. I can't remember with whom now. Just one-off, out of the pub. I'd possibly meet them at the pub, then have sex at the side of the road. I didn't know them, I was up for it…I look back now and think, "Oh, that was fun."

Mary, 94, from Norfolk, speaking about her sexual
awakening during the Second World War[17]

Gordon Gallup can't remember which sex shop he bought his plastic vagina from. It could have been California Exotic Novelties. Perhaps, though, it was Hollywood Erotique Novelties or Hollywood Exotic Novelties – all three are mentioned in his research. All three are – perhaps – equally unused to visits from distinguished psychology professors. What Professor Gallup does know is that his vagina was an excellent fit for the dildos that his students had bought, also from those sex shops.

"We got a very large cross-section of these different artificial genitals," he explains.

His experiment, The Human Penis as a Semen Displacement Device – if ever there was a psychology paper crying out to be turned into a pop song it's that – still required one final ingredient before it could be conducted. Semen.

For this, they enlisted three "sexually experienced males". Luckily for his graduate students, they – for, as ever in unpleasant scientific tasks, it was they – were not required to produce. Instead, they mixed up a concoction from corn-starch and tried different recipes, until all three were satisfied they had a liquid of the requisite viscosity.

Then, Professor Gallup says, they were ready to "load the vagina".[18]

The reason he was doing this was that he has a theory, about the shape of the penis. He thinks it's not only evolution's solution to inserting semen, but to removing it too. He thinks it acts as a pump, and that what it is doing is removing the sperm of competitors.

There are many strategies that men use to keep their wives and partners faithful – and vice versa. Sexual jealousy is the simplest. Getting them to wear a wedding ring is a more romantic adaptation. Forcing them to wear a burka and not go out unaccompanied is less so, but more effective. In an animal, the latter strategy would be called "mate-guarding" – some octopuses do something similar: they follow their females and strangle any males who come close (which leads weaker males to pretend to be females, in order to be able to sidle in unstrangled and unnoticed, and have cross-dressing sex).[19]

In many animals, though, such aggressive behaviour would only be the first line of defence. In some squirrels, who have an especially bracing sex life, the sperm also forms a seal

– called a mating plug – that prevents other male squirrels who follow from successfully copulating. It doesn't prevent the female squirrel from eating the mating plug if a more attractive male with more desirable genes hoves into view,[20] but it is better than nothing.

Fruit flies go even further. Their semen is far from a simple fluid. There is sperm in it, of course, but there are also chemicals that attack any rival sperm already there – and other chemicals that act as an anti-aphrodisiac, to convince the female to occupy herself more chastely afterwards.

These adaptations, collectively, are called "sperm competition" – and Professor Gallup thinks humans have them too. His proof is what happened to that cornstarch when his graduate students pushed the finest dildos Hollywood Exotique had to offer into the best vaginas from California Exotics – all of them, in his judgment, excellent analogues of the real thing.

With just one attempt, between 80 and 90 per cent of it was removed. So efficient was the suction that Professor Gallup is convinced that penises are designed for just this purpose.

This, then, would explain why humans, comparatively, take time having sex – with vigorous pumping (the word starts to take on a new meaning) as a prelude to the main event. "Obviously the longer the thrusting would last, the more effective," says Gallup, adding – in case this particular group of men didn't feel inadequate enough as it was – "You could view premature ejaculation as a potential failure to achieve semen displacement."

Gallup's work, and its interpretations, are not uncontroversial.* Critics have said it relies on assumptions that may not turn out to be correct. What happens, for instance, with men who keep going after ejaculation?[21]

Then there is one other assumption absolutely fundamental to his theory, which Darwin would take issue with. Sperm competition is only necessary if human women, like squirrels and fruit flies, are promiscuous.

That assumption is no longer a matter of significant discussion among Darwin's scientific descendants. Study after study has shown that, in the west, between 20 and 50 per cent of married women have affairs.[22] Before they get married, they have premarital sex. Most do so with one or more partners who will not become their husbands. They often, whisper it, enjoy it.

Ah but, critics counter, maybe this is a modern phenomenon, a consequence of the sexual revolution? If so, no one told that to the Empress Theodora.

In 527 AD, Theodora ascended to the Byzantine throne. History should remember her reign as a triumph of early feminism. Having begun a career working as a lowly actress, through cunning and charm she became one of the most powerful women the world has seen. What's more, she did not use that power just for herself. She passed rules against the trafficking of girls and liberalised the divorce laws in favour of women.

History should remember her for that, but history doesn't. Because if she was a feminist then, if the writer Procopius

---

* However, they are nowhere near as controversial as his work suggesting that semen might have antidepressant properties, making promiscuous women happier.

is to be believed, she was also what might be termed today a "sex-positive" one. "Though she flung wide three gates to the ambassadors of Cupid, she lamented that nature had not similarly unlocked the straits of her bosom, that she might there have contrived a further welcome to his emissaries,"* he wrote, in what was surely one of the greatest euphemisms of the classical age.

While Theodora's sexuality was a tool she had used to gain power, Procopius left readers in no doubt that it was also something she took unashamed pleasure in. Describing her acting days, he wrote, "Covered thus with a ribbon, she would sink down to the stage floor and recline on her back. Slaves to whom the duty was entrusted would then scatter grains of barley from above into the calyx of this passion flower, whence geese, trained for the purpose, would next pick the grains one by one with their bills and eat.

"When she rose, it was not with a blush, but she seemed rather to glory in the performance. For she was not only impudent herself, but endeavoured to make everybody else as audacious. Often when she was alone with other actors she would undress in their midst and arch her back provocatively, advertising like a peacock both to those who had experience of her and to those who had not yet had that privilege her trained suppleness."

Theodora was an outlier at the time – and also a key reason for Procopius' publishing success. His "Secret History" did not remain secret for terribly long. But she might not have been so unusual had she been born into a different society (aside from the geese bit. That would be unusual anywhere).

---

* Procopius also claims that the emperor Justinian could make his own head disappear. Some caution in interpretation may be required.

Similarly, consider the Ancient Greek play *Lysistrata*. Its plot is based on the premise that Greece's women withhold sexual privileges until their men stop fighting. This is, apparently, a clear manifestation of the idea that men want sex more than women – and it is in that part of their relationship that women hold the most power.

But see it performed and a far more nuanced picture emerges: the idea of a sex strike is not much fun for the women either and, contrary to Darwin's assertions, they are anything but coy about expressing that opinion. Take the scene where the women finally agree on their course of action. "OK," says Lysistrata, "we must give up the prick." Assent is not granted easily. Indeed, one of the wives responds, "Anything, anything you want. If I have to, I'll walk through fire. But not the prick. There's nothing like it, dearest Lysistrata."

Trying to establish our "true" nature, without the influence of cultural factors, is a fool's game. It leads to *reductio ad caveman* – a presumption that, as in the story of Plato's own cave, there is an ideal form of human hidden in our past that can tell us who we truly are. Culture can never be removed, and neither can our biology be explained in its absence. Even if we could see how our caveman ancestors behaved, this would not lead to a unifying theory of behaviour. There is no reason to presume those in the East African highlands would have had similar pressures and behaviour to those in the Rift Valley – let alone those later on shivering in caves in Europe.

Even so, if you want to see if current norms of behaviour are merely a fluke of our very specific western, industrial civilisation, then looking at other societies – in particular those removed from modern development – can be a useful way to assess our own "normality".

Among pre-industrial societies still in existence, almost half consider female premarital sex to be normal.[23] Some, such as the Na of China, consider it so normal they don't even have marriage[24] – women live with their brothers and relatives, and lovers are temporary nighttime interlopers. Others assume that wives will have had several sexual partners – and provide real-world evidence that doing so can be, evolutionarily speaking, a good idea. In the Namibian Himba tribe, where affairs are expected, women who are more promiscuous end up having more children and, crucially in the grand Darwinian calculus, more grandchildren.

What, then, of Darwin's coy females? Where do they fit in a world where it is conceivable that the penis has gone to the bother of evolving a pump just to counteract the amorous activity of rivals? And if that really is a possibility, why is it that women always claim to have so few sexual partners?

⁓ ⁓

The Mortimer Market Centre would be a lot like any of central London's NHS clinics, were it not for the massive stack of lube by reception. Down a dingy alleyway between Euston Station and Oxford Street, millions of people will have walked past it without noticing it – or the gaudy condom shop in its lobby. Walk in, past the HIV testing service, the contraceptive advice clinic and the lube, and on the top floor you will find the office from where Dame Anne Johnson monitors the state of Britain's love lives, the Sauron of sex.

Professor Johnson asks people questions about sex for a living. And quite probably the most important question she asks is, "How many sexual partners have you had?" She has never been completely satisfied with the response she has had over the years. In fact, she has written whole research papers on it.

The problem is, the mean number of lifetime heterosexual partners of women has to be the same as that for men. There is a very simple reason for this: by definition one of each is always involved in the act. It doesn't matter how you distribute that sex. It could be that one lucky woman has sex with each man in the country once, and no other woman has any sex at all. It could be that everyone pairs up monogamously for life. Either way, the average should be the same – in both those examples the average number of partners would be one.

So why is it not? Why do surveys always end up with the answer that women have fewer?

Professor Johnson is the principal investigator on Natsal, Britain's National Survey of Sexual Attitudes and Lifestyles. The survey, which is carried out every decade, is one of the largest in the world – with a representative sample of 15,000 adults quizzed for the last iteration in 2010. It was started in the 1980s in response to the AIDS crisis. She was part of a team trying to model how the disease would spread, and they soon realised they just did not have enough information to make even an educated guess.

"We needed data. We needed to know what kind of sex people were having with each other. Was it with or without a condom? What was their rate of sexual partner change?" she says. "So I suggested a random sample survey. They looked at me as if I was completely off my trolley. 'What, knock on people's doors and ask them about sex?'"

Her colleagues were not the only ones with their doubts.

Famously, Margaret Thatcher vetoed public funding for the survey, and they had to go to the Wellcome Trust. Quite why Thatcher was doubtful about it depends on who you ask, but it might not have been moral grounds. She was a scientist by training, she knew about the fuzziness of real-world data. Some think she just did not believe it would get useful results. Would people be honest?[25]

Professor Johnson was well aware of the difficulty of making it work. Every part of the survey was designed with the objective of getting people to tell the truth about something they rarely tell the truth about. Sometimes this involved thinking extremely carefully about apparently simple questions.

The first is the most basic. "What do you mean when you say 'sex'?" says Professor Johnson. This is an issue referred to in sex research as the Bill Clinton defence. "Everyone has a different view of what it was we were referring to. Oral, anal or vaginal?" Or how about homosexuality? "You would ask people if they were homosexual or heterosexual and they wouldn't know what it meant." They would assume that both were just some sort of recondite distinction between similar perversions. "'Homosexual? Heterosexual?' they would say, 'They're all queers.'"*

It is not just understanding the question that is crucial, it

---

* To see the effect of definition on response, you only have to look at the US National Survey of Family Growth, which interviewed 22,000 people between 2006 and 2010. It found that just under 2 per cent of men identified as gay, just over 1 per cent as bisexual. If this seems low, consider a third statistic: almost 6 per cent said they had had oral or anal sex with a man. Consider another statistic which highlights the plight of the pollster even more starkly: according to one legendary survey, when asked, 4 per cent of Americans said they had been decapitated.

is also important to get people to answer truthfully. People rarely do. To give an example: the average quantity of alcohol drunk per week in the UK, according to surveys, is around half the amount that leaves the shops. Unless a lot is spilled, people are telling their doctors what they think they want to hear.

To tackle this issue Alfred Kinsey, the pioneering 1940s and 1950s US sex researcher, used wording in his questions which minimised any interpretation that people were being judged, even when dealing with the most sensitive sexual practices. Rather than asking, for instance, if people had ever had an affair, he asked how old they were when they were first unfaithful – implying it was some sort of rite of passage rather than a moral Rubicon.

This approach led to some astonishing discoveries. Wardell Pomeroy, Kinsey's collaborator, wrote about an encounter with one interviewee.

"'How old were you the first time you ejaculated?' I asked him at one point.

"'14,' he answered.

"'How?' I asked.

"'With a horse,' I thought I heard him say.

"My mind went into high gear. The subject was telling me voluntarily about animal intercourse, and my instinct was to jump far ahead in the questioning and pursue the subject.

"'How often were you having intercourse with horses at fourteen?' I inquired. He seemed confused and taken aback, regarding me amazedly.

"'Well yes,' he said, 'it is true, I had intercourse with a pony at fourteen.'

"Later in the interview it developed that what he said was

'whores' not 'horse'. He thought I was a genius to have known somehow he had had intercourse with animals."[26]

The interviewee should not have been too ashamed, it turns out. Thanks to his careful line in questioning, Kinsey found that 8 per cent of men and 4 per cent of women had been in the same position. Although if you lived near a farm that more than doubled.[27]

Professor Johnson takes a simpler approach to removing social stigma. None of her team actually hears the answers to the questions. Instead, people write them down; originally by hand, and nowadays on a computer.

Yet even so, the difference in the sexes persists. Professor Johnson believes there are a few possible reasons for this. The first is that, despite their careful efforts to weight the data appropriately, the survey does not catch a full cross-section of society. Specifically, it misses out on one key demographic: prostitutes.

"I remember one of the interviewers saying they did knock on the door of a brothel," says Professor Johnson. She didn't have much luck. Bordellos, they have found, are not hugely open to visits by clipboard-wielding social scientists. This means that women with thousands of partners are excluded.

The second is that some people just can't remember.

One night in 2014, the actress Lindsay Lohan went out on the town. This was not, it must be said, in itself an event of great note. But on ending up in the bar of the Beverley Hills Hotel, she decided to make a list – and this became an event of such note that even today for legal reasons only half the list's contents are known. From the half we do know, number 21 is the singer Justin Timberlake. Number 24 is the actor Colin Farrell. Heath Ledger comes in at 25, the singer Adam Levine at number 30. The list stops at 36.

This list, which was retrieved by someone else in the bar after being discarded, is Lohan's collection of alleged "Hollywood Hookups". It is unusual not because it apparently implicates half of Hollywood's married A-listers in Lohan liaisons – most would accept that is not an Earth-shattering surprise. It is unusual, in Professor Johnson's view, for its specificity. Normally, when people reach that many conquests you see an odd pattern in the distribution.

"Sometimes, it requires calculation, they've got to figure it out," she said. "They say, 'Oh yeah, there was Mary, Jane, Susan, now Laetitia. And, oh yes, that girl while I was on leave during the war.' You can see in people's answers that estimation comes into it. At the upper end there is a bias towards round numbers: 25, 30, 35…" In other words, people are guessing, and when they guess they choose nice neat numbers.*

And it's not just guesswork that skews the answers. Crucially, people estimate in different ways, and with different ends in mind.

To understand why, you only have to think about how we view people with many partners. Sexually successful males are, in literature, Don Juans and Casanovas. Sexually successful females are, well, not "successful" at all.

When women were tried for witchcraft it was sometimes difficult to see whether it was them, or their sexuality, on trial. As these desperate women testified in front of pious (and prurient) men, they were forced to recount the times they had

---

* The same technique of statistical analysis shows that the election of Vladimir Putin is partially fixed. Over-zealous counting officers have had a tendency to make up big numbers, and there are spikes at 70 per cent of the vote, 75, 80, 85, 90, 95 – and 99. The last result was for Chechnya: a strong showing for a man who led a devastating war against the republic.

intercourse with Satan himself – this leading to stern documents recounting the idiosyncratic biology of the Dark One's penis. Doubtless Professor Gallup would be fascinated to perform a study on the evolutionary utility of Lucifer's forked penis (according to one "witch's" account) and "intolerably cold" ejaculate.* Throughout history, women's sexuality has been policed, and even pathologised. The term nymphomaniac was created for just this purpose.

Professor Johnson says that this remains relevant today. "What's the female equivalent of a stag? It's a slut," she says. She thinks women subconsciously interpret their sexual history in a way that lessens their promiscuity. "They would be more likely to say, 'That one didn't really count.'" With the same real-life total of 13, men might round up to 15, women might round down to ten.

So heterosexual women do indeed have the same number of sexual partners as men – that is a mathematical truism. But it is increasingly clear they just don't admit it, possibly even to themselves. Professor Johnson is keen to distinguish between this and lying. "If people trust you enough to tell you about their sex life you shouldn't accuse them of lying. I prefer to say, 'not report accurately'." This may be so, but in a small study psychologists showed that when you wire women up to lie-detecting machines, then ask how many sexual partners they have had, the number matches that of men – and exceeds the one they gave when not wired up to the detector, even when assured of absolute anonymity.[28]

---

* Not all witches were so down on Beelzebub. One inquisitor said that his investigations had led him to conclude that Satan's member was "extremely fleshy" and witches who encountered it "for several days afterward remain worn out".

Does the same social pressure that makes women under-estimate also make men overestimate? If women say to themselves, "That one didn't really count," would the man they were with in the same encounter go for the opposite interpretation?

As I talk to Professor Johnson, I realise that I was a subject of her survey. In 1999, a nice woman came round to my family home, asked who lived there and selected me.

My mum, a maths teacher who enjoys seeing how surveys work, asked to sit in. It was politely suggested that that was a bad idea.

So we went into the dining room, and the woman turned a laptop towards me and asked me to fill the survey in. As I was a 17-year-old at an all-boys grammar school which made us wear suits and work on Saturday mornings, most of the questions were, sadly I felt, not relevant to me. I rapidly clicked through.

A few minutes later I turned the laptop back round, complete. "That was quick," she said. The unspoken implication hung there. It still smarts.

⌣‿⌣

If we can't trust people, what do we trust? Well, while Professor Gallup's pumps are certainly an interesting bit of anatomical evidence, the most reliable judge of female prom-iscuity is located somewhere else.

Because there is one final evidential nugget that tells a story of female promiscuity better than any cross-cultural survey or psychology experiment: testicles.

Silverback gorillas are the ultimate alpha males. They are

big, muscly, and control a harem of females – won in combat. And they have tiny, tiny balls. Chimpanzee males, however, are physically much less imposing, and have to woo each female anew, sharing her with a succession of suitors. Are they emasculated by this? That's one interpretation – but it does mean they have massive balls.

Testicle size in a species is a pretty good proxy for female promiscuity. If you are a scary silverback with no concerns about infidelity, then you don't need to waste time making sperm. You have competed before getting down to sex, using your strength, and the competition has scampered back into the forest, defeated. If you are a chimpanzee, however, the competition is something that happens not before sex but during it – not with the size of your muscles but with the volume of your sperm. They make love, not war – except that for them making love is a kind of war, where their semen drowns out the competition by sheer numbers.

And where do humans fit in this? Well, our testicles are not the size of gorillas'. Sure, they're not the size of chimpanzees' either. But ours are not monogamous testicles. At least on the basis of male anatomy, we can conclude that female humans are regularly unfaithful to their partners today, and they always have been.

Rather than sitting around chastely, saving themselves until they have chosen a good provider to give them babies, they seem to persist in consistently taking more than one partner. All of which presents a difficulty.

Why would this be so? After all, given the consequences of sex with an unsuitable partner are so much graver for them, they have far less to gain. But the more people have studied male and female sexuality, the more they have realised that it is rarely as simple as that. Some feminist researchers have gone further. They have argued that there has been a wilful blindness in the community, which has studied all the factors that might affect male evolution, but ignored those affecting females – especially if they involve female agency.

Sarah Hrdy,* a US primatologist, was one of the first to make this case – after noting in her observations of our closest relatives that they often did not do what they were meant to. Between "brazenly assertive macaques" and "the not-so-coy solicitations of neighbouring males by 'harem-dwelling' langurs", primates just didn't seem to obey the rules.

Yes, the males were ardent, but the females were often not as coy as they should have been. Yet still, among her colleagues, she said, "The old ditty 'Hoggamus higgamous; Men are polygamous; Higgamus, hoggamous women monogamous" was elevated from a witty summary of the double standard into a profound and universal truth about Nature generally, and human nature in particular."

There is one important reason (of, as it turns out, many) why women might have sexual strategies that are more complicated than simply waiting for Mr Right to come along. That reason is that whether they end up with Mr Right, Mr Goodenough or even Mr Time-to-Settle, they will still hold a great advantage in the marital calculus. While men are not able to trick women into bringing up an unrelated child, women are able to trick men into doing so. And, sometimes, that is a very good idea.

Imagine, for a moment, that a woman has chosen a lovely man. Reliable, good company, decent job – but not exactly

---

* By some distance the most prominent primatologist to have no vowels in her name.

with the chiselled jawline and smouldering eyes of a Mills and Boon hero. He is probably the sort of man who spent his frustrating teenage years having girls describe him as "nice". Possibly while going to an all-boys grammar school.

Imagine too that she has the opportunity to sleep with a living, breathing version of said chiselled smoulderer, but only for one night – before, fertilised and fortified, returning to domesticity. She gets the paternal investment of reliable, nice husband, and the angular jawbones of a Christian Grey-style cad. And when they grow up, her sons, secretly bolstered with his rakish genes, can go forth and multiply through the same strategy – cads themselves. The creeps shall inherit the Earth.*

Obviously this is a simplification – it is perfectly possible for people to both smoulder and, say, hold down a steady job in accountancy. But even so, it is a trope that appears time and time again – whether in the lady of the manor romping with the muscled stable boy or a princess finding herself a nice dashing cavalry officer.

And there is some evidence of it beyond anecdote. Some research has found that when women look for short-term sexual partners, they are more likely to go for muscular men with symmetrical faces and v-shaped torsos. They increase their standards.[29] If that seems only sensible – who would have an affair with someone who isn't even better than the

---

* Note that it is not even necessary for chiselled smoulderers to be finer specimens of manhood, in the sense they are better able to hunt, gather and evade sabre-tooth tigers. It is enough that women desire chiselled genes for chiselled genes to be desirable. Famously, evolutionists have argued that the peacock's tail isn't useful. But if peacocks with lovely tails get more peahens, then increasingly flamboyant tails will be selected.

alternative at home? – then you're probably a woman. In the same situation men, conversely, lower theirs – a fact that may or may not be comforting for wives with straying husbands.[30,] *

As far as Professor Gallup is concerned, even this is only part of the picture. For women already a few babies down, a bit of variety is worthwhile enough that they can relax their quality control – and go for different men.

"By the time a woman has had three children all sired by the same male, she will have sampled 87.5 per cent of his genes," he says. "Which means that any subsequent children sired by that man will be increasingly genetically redundant. Genetic variability among children is a hedge against an uncertain future."

However, none of this implies that people know, on a conscious level, what they are up to. No woman has ever given birth and thought, "Right, that's 87.5 per cent of his genes sampled, time for some cuckolding." There are mechanisms, long established, by which our minds and bodies can guide our actions – and the next chapters will look at the more potent of these mechanisms: hormones.

Because people don't have to consciously make a decision to actually make a decision. And no man has to know why, to return to another theme of Professor Gallup's, he feels especially affectionate towards his wife after returning from a business trip.

"A common saying is that absence makes the heart grow fonder," says the professor, espousing his wider relationship philosophy. "The reason is nothing to do with romanticism."

---

* This is not the only situation where men lower their standards. A 2017 paper found, gloriously, "Men with a terminal illness relax their criteria for facial attractiveness".

Of course not. "The reason is, absence provides the opportunity for female infidelity." After an absence, he maintains, your heart feels fonder, if you are a man at least, because you need to make love quickly – in case there is a need for some serious sperm competition.

How does his wife feel about that? "She approves of most of my analysis." It must take a special woman to be married to an evolutionary psychologist. "I don't know," he replies, ever the empiricist, "I don't have a control group."

3

MARS

Man red in tooth and claw

Under the spreading chestnut tree
The village smithy stands
The smith a gloomy man is he
McCormick has his glands.

Traditional (ish)

It was not the surgery that changed Sam Schweiger's life, he says now. It was the hormones.

Schweiger already knew how women thought; he had spent the first 35 years of his life living as one – called Sabine. Then he received his first shot of testosterone and suddenly, he says, he understood men too.

"It's when I realised women and men are talking separate languages...they don't understand each other. They are..." he hesitates to say it, to make the obvious point – then relents. "It is like Mars and Venus."

For female-to-male transsexuals, testosterone has a physical role – the same physical role it performs in people born male. It makes them become hairy and strong, and helps them look like the sex they have chosen to become.

But if you chat to people who have made the transition, they say that is just the start of it. "The first day you get it, it's an explosion," says Schweiger. "You think, 'Wow, where do I put all these hormones?'" Beforehand they are warned about the effect on their libido, but it was still a shock. "It's so different. Now I knew why men are acting like that, why men go in a sexual direction."

It went deeper than just sex. The way Sam thought about the world changed. "I always felt guilty before. I had lots of fears – I was really emotional as a woman. And then you get your first shot and wow. Everything changes. I became really confident. I started to become calmer and relaxed. I had more energy, more power."

He realised that his relationships with his female friends had changed. "They are always talking, always want to discuss. It's not interesting for me any more – I don't want to discuss."

"Sometimes women are a bit afraid to raise their voice or become more aggressive in a discussion," he says. Not for him any more. "Now it's no problem."

For the first weeks of an embryo's development, males and females are indistinguishable. Then around the eighth week, when the embryo is just an inch long, there is a divergence. In those with a Y chromosome, testes develop. These produce a surge of a chemical, made up of 19 carbon atoms, 28 hydrogen atoms and two oxygen atoms: testosterone.

Later in life, boys will experience other surges in

testosterone. They will find it rises when they have sex, watch pornography or even talk to an attractive woman.[31] They will find that it falls when they look after children, marry or suffer failures.[32] Although if that failure is a divorce, testosterone levels will return to those of a singleton – urging them back onto the dating market.

There is evidence, albeit disputed, that rapists have more of it.[33] So too, though, do better dancers.[34] It will track their successes, and failures – even vicariously. During the 2008 presidential election in the US, scientists measured testosterone in supporters of both candidates. When Barack Obama won, its levels in male Republican voters fell.[35]

Girls have testosterone too, although not in the same quantities. But the way it works in them is instructive. Those who receive more of it in the womb later behave in more stereotypical masculine ways. They choose more "male" toys, and engage in more rough play.[36] It is the invisible chemical that is the variable, not the visible gender. Testosterone seems to have made them more "male".*

Testosterone, in the popular consciousness, is the man hormone. It is the chemical that makes men fight, makes markets crash, and powers the grand game of sexual competition that urges men on to make the finest art, the most beautiful music and commit the most terrible crimes. Where there are differences in how the sexes approach sex, testosterone is the first place researchers look. But is that fair?

Given how recently testosterone was discovered, it is astonishing how rapidly this cultural trope has taken hold.

---

* However, testosterone is still important for all women. And in males some testosterone is converted to oestrogen – it is not simply a male hormone.

Testicles themselves have been associated with masculinity since classical times.[37] Today, you swear an oath by placing your hand on your heart or on a bible. In ancient Rome, you went into court and placed your hand instead "on the seat of manliness" – cupping your toga like a Sicilian preparing to defend his family's honour.[38]

It wasn't until the Enlightenment that scientists began to contest this manliness-seat theory.

In 1849 Arnold Berthold, a Danish professor, began experiments on capons, the cockerel version of eunuchs. Capons are, like eunuchs, fatter, docile and more subdued. In eunuchs, this makes for an excellent harem guard. In capons, it makes for an excellent source of chicken nuggets. What happens if you transplant the testicles of virile roosters into the emasculated, but tastier, capons? Well, their comb gets redder, their muscle mass firms up, and they regain, at least temporarily, their cock-a-doodle-do.

Why stop at cockerels, though? Certainly for French physiologist Charles-Edouard Brown-Séquard, this research line was far too promising to restrict to birds. So in his early seventies, and impotent, he decided to inject himself with extract of dog testes. In an 1889 lecture at the Société de Biologie in Paris, he excitedly reported the results – and they were so successful, he told the audience, that that very morning he had "paid a visit" to Mme Brown-Séquard.*

---

*   Brown-Séquard's true scientific successor is Sir Giles Skey Brindley, a urologist. In 1983 he gave a lecture on a new treatment he had devised for erectile dysfunction. Years later, Laurence Klotz, an attendee, recounted what happened next. "He then summarily dropped his trousers and shorts, revealing a long, thin, clearly erect penis. There was not a sound in the room. Everyone had stopped breathing.

    "But the mere public showing of his erection from the podium was

Alas for the madame, and her plucky husband, the results did not persist. He attributed the apparent success instead to "*espérance absurde*" – wishful thinking.

Not that this put off those who came later – most notably Victor Lespinasse, a Chicago surgeon who, as the *New York Times* put it, was the "dean of gland transplantation" and the author of the saying "A man is as old as his glands".[39] A *bon mot* that has, inexplicably, been lost to history.

Lespinasse made a reputation by hanging around executions, whipping out the deceased's testicles while still warm, and inserting these criminal gonads in paying clients. Such was his apparent success that in 1922 a very special client discreetly approached him. Harold McCormick was a scion of the McCormick family, who had made their fortune selling agricultural equipment. Then about to turn 50, McCormick had just ridded himself of a wife from an even richer family – the Rockefellers – and was looking to bring the vigour of youth to the bed of his new amour. So he asked Lespinasse if he could help – in confidence.

Unfortunately for him, the Chicago press was no respecter of confidences, and, with considerable glee, they found out. A rumour took hold that the testicles came from a blacksmith. That led to a verse being composed. "Under the spreading

---

not sufficient. He paused, and seemed to ponder his next move. The sense of drama in the room was palpable. He then said, with gravity, 'I'd like to give some of the audience the opportunity to confirm the degree of tumescence.' With his pants at his knees, he waddled down the stairs, approaching (to their horror) the urologists and their partners in the front row. As he approached them, erection waggling before him, four or five of the women in the front rows threw their arms up in the air, seemingly in unison, and screamed loudly. The scientific merits of the presentation had been overwhelmed, for them, by the novel and unusual mode of demonstrating the results."

chestnut tree/The village smithy stands/The smith a gloomy man is he/McCormick has his glands."

If only he had waited. In the same city, a new approach was being pioneered – that involved no criminal or blacksmith gonad implantations at all.

In 1927, a University of Chicago professor called Fred Koch got his hands on 20kg of bull testicles. Rather than inserting them into hapless patients, he decided to extract their quintessence. With the help of his students, he then mashed them and fractionated them to distil down a few grams of a long-fabled substance – the chemical essence of man. In his hands he believed he had the concentrated liquid potency of the testicle. But was it the substance they were looking for? Carefully, they injected it into capons and waited.

Among his previously docile flock the cocks crowed again. The science of testosterone was dawning.

·–·

I have Koch to thank for the small brown package that arrives on my doorstep one morning. Heavily taped up, with a return address in an Indian light industrial estate that probably doesn't exist, it contains ten small sachets of a product called androgel. Testosterone supplements tend to have names like that. Fortesta, Viromone, Testoviron, they evoke images of virility, of manly conquest.

They are sold – the grey-market versions at least – on websites showing muscly men doing muscly things, and doubtless returning home with sufficient muscles to whisk off a swooning virgin and prove their newfound muscly stamina.

My wife does not swoon as I take my shirt off and rub the

gel as instructed onto my back (the instructions also warn, several times, not to apply it anywhere lower). Instead, she complains. "Am I about to find that the man I married isn't nice at all, but just low in hormones?"

The legitimate market for testosterone supplements is not muscly men looking to seduce women. It is men with a medical problem that means they are low in testosterone. With too little of the hormone, they can feel tired, suffer a greater risk of heart conditions[40] and have sexual problems. For men in the normal range, supplementation is not advised. But prescriptions for older men have still doubled in the UK in the past decade, and trebled in the US.

Even if you can't get a prescription, all is not lost. Provided, that is, you are prepared to download a browser that lets you access the darknet, buy a piece of software that lets you pretend you are in Russia, use a bitcoin exchange that circumvents money-laundering checks, and then visit a marketplace where everything, from Uzis to heroin, is a commodity.

The package arrives two weeks later, and after applying it I button up my shirt and head into work.

I am not sure what to expect. Men with higher testosterone are more likely to buy and sell stolen goods, be arrested and use weapons in fights.[41] When they are in the military, they are more likely to end up in a combat situation.[42] There are sadly limited opportunities for such behaviour in the offices of *The Times*. Nevertheless, I am the only person in the building (who I know of) who is currently illegally taking a drug. So there's that.

Can my colleagues spot it, though? Can they tell that, emanating from the crust of gel slowly drying on my back, the essence of manliness is circulating in my system? Physically

they probably can't – although behaviourally they may – but that does not mean that people do not have ways to spot it over the long run.

Take Egill, for example. Egill was an exemplary Viking. Good at pillaging? Absolutely. Not averse to a bit of raping? Well, Norsemen will be Norsemen. Able to hold his own in a fight? Naturally – he committed his first murder as a child, and his last on his deathbed. As Tarrin Wills, a University of Aberdeen linguist and historian, puts it, "Egill had a lifelong love of homicide."

And yet, there is a contradiction here – because after the campaigning is done, the English monasteries ravaged, what happens when he gets home? "A good Viking should be aggressive, dominant, go abroad and rape and pillage," says Dr Wills. "But the kinds of guys who are good at rape and pillage are not very good husbands and farmers."

So he has a theory. He thinks that the Icelandic sagas recounting Egill's heroic exploits (sample exploit: at the age of seven he was cheated in a game of cards, so he got an axe and split the skull of his opponent to his teeth) are really a Viking *Crimewatch* – warning women of the kind of men to avoid, for marriage, if not for a wild temporary liaison.

The reason for this theory is the attention paid to particular features. "They describe legendary warriors in terms of width of their foreheads, heavy eyebrows or beards and receding hairlines. All these things are known to be indicators of high testosterone but it is highly unusual for men to be depicted in this way in literature from this period," says Dr Wills.

Egill in particular is shown to have "very distinctive features, with a wide forehead...his beard grew over a long part of his face and his chin and entire jaw were very broad...

he became harsh-looking and fierce when angry". In another saga, the link is even clearer. "A man hears a description of a group of men coming to attack him," Dr Wills said. "For each of the men, the level of these physical testosterone indicators predicts the level of violence."

He came across the connection while reading a paper about City traders – the modern-day-equivalent marauding Nordic chieftains. It explicitly described the same physiological traits among the more aggressive bankers, an echo of the Icelandic sagas a millennium on. He could have equally read other modern studies, which specifically look at the attractiveness or otherwise of high-testosterone men.

They find the contradiction at the heart of Egill's tale. As might be expected, more masculine features are more attractive – who wouldn't want to sire the kind of son who could ravage the coastline of Northumberland? – but women also associate them with aggression, manipulativeness and selfishness.[43] As well they might. Men higher in testosterone are less likely to marry, and more likely to divorce or have affairs if they do.[44] They make worse parents and are less tuned to the cries of infants.[45]

And me? The problem is, although there are no babies around to test the crying theory, I definitely don't feel especially aggressive at work. I queue happily for the coffee machine, I suffer no urge to have a sexual dalliance in the stationery cupboard. There is another science writer on the paper, arguably my direct competition, but I feel neither the need to engage in a dominance contest with him, nor to hump him.

Then there are my actual enemies, the news desk, whose job it is to make me write about things I don't want to write about. This should surely make me more aggressive towards them. Why, I ask one of the home news editors who knows about my experiment, have I not punched him? He more than deserves it. "If it helps, I think you've filed more muscular prose today," he says, consolingly. It is hardly leading a war party on the next cave, and taking their women for my harem, though, is it?

Why are the effects not clearer? In animals, the experiments linking testosterone to aggression do not stop at cockerels. If you castrate a stag, for instance, it will not fight. Inject it with testosterone, and it will.[46] The chemical makes mice mean, and rats ratty.

The days when you could create eunuchs for science are past, alas, but there are other less precise methods for scientifically testing the effect of testosterone in humans – without taking my ethically dubious route of using supplements.

In one ingenious psychological experiment, the researchers manipulated men's testosterone levels by allowing them to hold a gun (it really can be that simple). Then the men played a game against an unseen opponent – and when they won were allowed to add variable amounts of hot sauce to their opponent's water. In those whose testosterone levels rose, so did the sheer bloodyminded willingness to make their opponent drink chilli water.[47]

Why have I not noticed this surge of bullishness in myself? Before I even took the supplement, I had visited an illegal website that sells sniper rifles and sex – if holding a gun raises testosterone, surely that should too. The truth is, for an idea so culturally entrenched, the scientific evidence showing that testosterone actually does turn men into Egills is a bit more confusing – and a lot more interesting.

In 2016, psychologists injected men with testosterone and

made them play a game in which they had to share money, and could reward or punish people on the basis of how it was shared. If they disliked their opponent they could fine him, but they themselves would incur a fifth of the fine. If they liked their opponent they could reward him – but again at a cost of a fifth of the reward. Those who thought they were getting an unfairly small share of the money were, as expected, more likely to punish the other players after the injection. But, the converse was true. If they had a fair share, they were more likely to reward.[48]

Testosterone made them nice, but it also made them nasty. What was going on?

Similar apparent paradoxes can be seen outside of the laboratory. In 2004, a study was published after psychiatrists followed the same group of boys from the age of nine until 15. During this period, they all experienced one of the great testosterone surges of a male's life – puberty.

With its arrival, there was a corresponding rise in antisocial behaviour – but only in those boys who had naughty peers. In those who did not, the testosterone was instead correlated with positive leadership behaviour. In both situations, more testosterone meant boys did more of the sort of thing that gave them status. It's just that in one case it was glue sniffing behind the bike sheds, and in the other it was joining the debating team.[49]

For much of the time we have known about testosterone, we have been getting it wrong. Testosterone doesn't make you aggressive, it makes you status-seeking.* Sometimes that

---

* This does not mean women don't also fight for status, but there is evidence it is a more complicated, social process – with different causes. See later chapters.

means aggression but it needn't. If you measure testosterone levels in chess players, for instance, you will find them elevated before a match. You will find them even more elevated after, if they win. They don't then tip over the board and head off to the pub to glass someone in a heated argument about the Nimzo-Indian Defence.

If you measure testosterone in men in general, it will help you predict their likelihood of taking risks. Its peaks match corresponding peaks in deaths, as those risks translate into mortality – with men heading off to war, clambering up mountains, paragliding off them or just driving too fast.[50] At all ages, boys and men are more likely to suffer a fireworks injury. Between the ages of ten and 55 the difference is so great that men are never less than three times as likely to end up in hospital after mucking around with fireworks.[51] Men are two or three times more likely to suffer a major head injury, young men are five times more likely.[52] At all ages men die more.[53]

Testosterone is, the argument goes, a way of making men take the sort of risks or make the sort of sacrifices necessary to compete for status. Then, by surging again after they are successful, it encourages them to do so again. The causation goes both ways – competition comes from it and leads to it. It is not hard to see why a chemical that encourages riskier behaviour just after risky behaviour has paid off may be undesirable on a stock market.

Not that bankers necessarily agree. On the day I choose to take my supplement, I have a meeting scheduled with a neuroscientist who has been conducting a study into how journalists cope with stress. As part of this process, two months earlier I had a blood test that measured, among other things, my testosterone level. It was low, although within the normal range. At our meeting she tells me this is likely because I have two young children. Men who take on their share of parenting experience a drop in testosterone, all the better to attune to their babies' cries presumably.

She disapproves of my experiment, but it does not surprise her as much as I had thought it would. "I have several clients who take supplements," she says. Much of her work is with big financial companies, helping their teams cope with stress.

Sometimes they tell her that they are taking illegal testosterone, precisely because it will help them be less cautious. "They also think it will help their muscles," she says. They've clearly been on the same websites as me.

Maybe they will take more risks. Maybe that will even be good for their careers (if not the economy in the long run). A 2008 study found that by measuring testosterone levels in City traders you could predict their profitability over the day.[54]

That said, the link between testosterone and another career choice is far better established – crime. Violent crime is, overwhelmingly, perpetrated by males – and, with the exception of sexual crime and domestic violence, it is also overwhelmingly experienced by males. Across history and geography, men are brutes. In the UK, 80 per cent of violent crime is committed by men. The same is true, or worse, in all countries: 93 per cent of all inmates in the US are male.[55] The most violent of those prisoners (interestingly, this goes for women too) have the highest testosterone.

If testosterone is, at least some of the time, so unpleasant, if it causes financial crises, if it makes men risk themselves in pointless fights over pointless insults – if it ultimately makes more men die while seeking status, then why have it at all? Why might status be so important for men? The answer is because from an evolutionary perspective there is one thing just as bad as dying: not having children. And this idea led to one of the most important theories in modern biology, known as Bateman's principle.

In 1948 a scientist called Angus Bateman organised some fruit fly orgies. Each of the fruit flies had been inbred to ensure they had particular mutations – meaning that when they reproduced the parentage of the offspring could be spotted. So if a fruit fly had, for instance, hairier wings, then they knew it came from the hairy-winged father.

Over the course of six fruit fly free-for-alls, Bateman established two crucial things. Firstly, the more mates a male fruit fly had, the more offspring he had. For females this was not the case – unsurprisingly, since the female will only get pregnant once at a time. Secondly, there was more variance in success among the males than in the females. Some, the rock stars of the fruit fly world, did very well. Others did not.

In the past decade a dispute has emerged about the rigour of his experiments, but not about the general principles involved. In the 60 years since, similar observations have been made across the animal world. In 2016 a review of the entire literature investigated how the principle held up in 66 species, from frogs to fish. The scientists found that every species was different but, again and again, the least investing sex – normally the male – had the most variation in sexual success. Some did well, some did badly. Males benefited by being indiscriminate, females by being less so. The theories, they said, "provide a powerful explanation for differences between males and females".[56, *]

More pertinently, perhaps, the same seems to be true in the 66th species considered by the scientists: humans.[57] Across human societies, there is a greater variation in the number of children men have compared to women. This is true everywhere, researchers have found, from the openly polygamous hunter-gatherer societies of modern-day Africa to the strictly religious, strictly monogamous ones of 18th-century Finland.

We humans live in polygamous societies, and always have done. Sometimes, this is obvious. It would have been very clear to the hundreds of men in, say, Istanbul, who could not get wives while the sultan had a massive harem. It would also have been obvious to our distant ancestors. Recent analysis has found that, around the start of agriculture, there was an astonishing genetic bottleneck. For every one man who reproduced, 17 women did. That means 16 hung around jealously watching the chieftain impregnate half the village. Seventeen is quite a size, for the average harem.[58]

The situation is similar today: some successful men still have more than one wife, but usually not concurrently. Hence we tend not to notice it as much in the western world.

---

* Oddly, there is a coda to Bateman's work. The 2016 paper was partly prompted by the failed attempts to replicate his experiments. People have looked at the statistics and methods he used more closely, and found them wanting. One of the founding studies of the evolution of sexuality appears to be shaky, and if this had been known at the time, research may well have taken a different route. It wasn't, though, so biologists instead spent 60 years investigating whether it held up in other species. And it did. Ironically it is just possible that fruit flies, who kicked this all off, might not have such simple evolutionarily determined sex roles, and good on the fruit fly sisterhood if so. But most other animals do.

Consider, for instance, Rod Stewart. The singer's first child, a girl, was born in 1963, when he was just 17. At the age of 66, when she was 48 – and at the end of her reproductive life – he had his eighth child, from his fifth partner. Six months later that son, in one of those logic problems that are best not to overthink, welcomed the arrival of his own niece.

By taking extra partners, younger than him, Stewart has remained reproductive into his 70s – and, to use the brute logic of evolution, has along the way ensured other less successful men have been deprived of fertile women.

Men are far more likely to have a second family than women. They are more likely to get remarried after divorce, and when they do are likely to go for someone a decade younger than their first wife.[59] Men in the Forbes 400 rich list have wives on average seven years younger than them. They have second wives on average 22 years younger.[60]

So if we shifted the parameters and looked at the number of wives a man has in his life, even though they are not concurrent, then it could be concluded that we still display the traits of a polygamous society.*

And while this is lovely for Stewart, it is bad news for other men. In a polygamous society, women are never short of a man. They may have to share him, but if they are fertile they will always have a baby. A plain woman without status will still reproduce. A boring man with no money, however, will

---

* It is possible to be effectively polygamous without even having sex with another woman. Wealthy families used to take nursemaids as standard. Since lactating women are generally unable to conceive, the wealthy mother shortened the possible intervals between her pregnancies by effectively "stealing" a portion of the nursemaid's fertility. In this way, the two women enabled the man to increase his stock, even though his wife was the only one he slept with.

not. At the same time as the Stewarts of the world bed women younger than their daughters a rejected man's genetic offering – an unbroken line of reproduction stretching back to the first life on earth – will abruptly stop. Men, even today, are more likely to be childless than women.

This makes it a lot more important for men than women to compete, at least when it comes to mating.

There is a temptation to take a simple explanatory idea, such as the need for men to compete for mates, and extend it to become a rubric for human society. Is their competitiveness why men earn more? Is it why there are more male prime ministers, why there are more CEOs called John than CEOs with breasts?

Perhaps. The problem is this mating-based explanation does not merely predict that men will be more competitive than women. It has very little to say about female competitiveness at all. Yet, women clearly do compete. Sometimes they do so viciously, as anyone who has witnessed the politics of adolescent friendship groups would attest.*

And while men may take more risks of the physical kind – mortality statistics are proof of that, and even the strongest of feminist arguments find it difficult to argue with a cemetery – those are not the only kind of risks. Try telling a woman

---

* In the excellently titled "Queen Bees and Wannabes", Rosalind Wiseman describes the horrors of the adolescent popularity game – presided over by the one "Queen Bee". "Through a combination of charisma, force, money, looks, will, and social intelligence, this girl reigns supreme over the other girls and weakens their friendships with others, thereby strengthening her own power and influence."

looking for bread for her starving child that there is no evolutionary incentive for females to compete for resources. Complex human behaviours are rarely simply explained – and, beyond those involving sex, I am not attempting to do so in this book.*

After a day absorbing testosterone from my shoulders, I would be lying if I said I could identify any effects beyond unpleasant-feeling shoulders. Probably, though, given my testosterone is already in the normal range, and I only had one day of supplements anyway, any major personality changes would be attributable to the "*espérance absurde*" error of Monsieur Brown-Séquard.

Was that an error being made by Sam Schweiger too, in how he interpreted the emotional changes after becoming a man? Certainty is a luxury that science can rarely achieve. There are almost always other explanations – however compelling the tale. Consider Schweiger's situation.

Schweiger had been living in what he considered to be the wrong body. Then, over a short period of time, it became the right body. He looked in the mirror and saw the person he wanted to be. He began to look like a man, and be treated like a man. Is it surprising that he would also feel a bit more like a stereotypical man? It is difficult to imagine a situation with the potential to create a stronger placebo effect.

Yet Georg Kranz is pretty sure that is not all that is going on, and has evidence to prove it. Dr Kranz had been researching depression when he met Schweiger. Depression is one of those persistent gender differences in the brain that are

---

* For an extensive, and often entertaining, critique of wider behavioural interpretations of testosterone's effects, read *Testosterone Rex* by Cordelia Fine.

difficult to ascribe purely to cultural conditioning. Women are far more likely to be depressed, while men for their part are more likely to be autistic.

Dr Kranz was interested in the part that hormones might play in that. "When hormones fluctuate, the mood fluctuates," he says. "This becomes quite clear when you look at syndromes like postpartum depression."

What about male hormones? He realised that female-to-male transsexuals were an ideal natural experiment – an intervention of the kind that would otherwise be impossible. So Schweiger, and 17 others going through the same transition, agreed to work with him.

Most had experiences very similar to Schweiger's. "Sexual desire significantly increased. They told me they suddenly really wanted sex, that they were really attracted towards their partner," says Dr Kranz. In an interview in *Cosmopolitan*, another female-to-male transsexual said, "I think the increase in sex drive surprised me the most. I knew it would happen, but I still didn't expect it to be that strong. Masturbation turned from a fun activity to an everyday necessity."

As with Schweiger, it doesn't stop there. Dr Kranz says the other subjects started getting worse body odour, they felt the cold less. And, they claimed, they thought about life differently.

"It's really very stereotypical almost. There's a sex stereotype that males don't think too much, that when they have a problem they follow one solution and stick to it – whereas females weigh the pros and cons. This is exactly what they told me happened to them.

"They said they couldn't understand their female friends any more. They said after therapy they cannot appreciate these lengthy chats with them about social relationships. The proneness to weep, to cry, was reduced."

That was not what convinced Dr Kranz of testosterone's effects, though. Because at the same time as he was speaking to them about the changes, he was also scanning their brains. Consistently, he saw the same thing. Two parts of the brain related to language shrank, but the connections between them strengthened. Something was happening in the parts of the brain responsible for verbal fluency – a trait that is measurably different in men and women – and it was happening in the same way in those who received the hormones.[61]

Of course, it could be that the brain changed in the same way because they all had such a similar experience – and it was the social experience making the change rather than the testosterone. But Dr Kranz isn't convinced. The brain has hormone receptors, there was a surge of hormones – and here was a verifiable structural change. At some point, it becomes simpler just to blame the hormone.

"In the end we can't see for certain how the hormones affect the system. But I think we have a pretty good argument to assume the hormonal therapy was responsible for these changes," he said. "The most parsimonious explanation* is that the hormones did it."

None of this will convince everyone, but the evidence that testosterone affects the brain is difficult to explain away – even if saying precisely how is harder.

Schweiger, too, is in no doubt about the effects of testosterone. Those experiments that began a century ago with ground-up bull testicles and transplanted cockerel gonads

---

* Scientists say "parsimonious" when they mean "simplest". Ironically.

have changed his life – in a way that would have been completely impossible before. Through testosterone, he has become an ambassador between the sexes.

"I'm really happy I was born that way, so I know both sides of the gender world," he says. He realises that this gift is fading, though. The longer the gap between his old life and his new one, the less Schweiger can remember what it was to be a woman, and live in a body with very different hormones – with, as the next chapter explores, a very different rhythm. "Before testosterone it was clear to me how women act and think," he says. "But I am losing it. With every year that passes I lose a bit of my understanding of them."

4

VENUS

The benefits of promiscuity; the deceptiveness of fertility

Consider, of what importance to society the chastity of women is. Upon that all the property in the world depends. We hang a thief for stealing a sheep; but the unchastity of a woman transfers sheep, and farm and all, from the right owner.
Samuel Johnson, from *The Life of Johnson*, Volume 5

If women were baboons, it would be so much simpler.

For most of the time, female baboons go about their business untroubled by sex. They forage alone, avoid hyenas, dig up roots. Then, when they are fertile they experience a rush of hormones, their bottom inflates, they display a bright-red posterior to impress their suitors – and they temporarily leave the foraging to one side to mate.

In this way, no baboon need ever bother with pointless sex.

Yet sadly in humans, for men looking for an easier way to understand the dating market, this doesn't happen to women. Unlike other primates, women feel little urge to display their bottoms when fertile, and even those that do don't actively inflate them beforehand. Women have, to use the biological term, "concealed ovulation": neither they nor their partners can easily tell when they are fertile.

Quite why signs of fertility have been lost in humans has been the subject of much debate among biologists. Is it a means of keeping men interested, and investing in their offspring, long term? Could it be, a less misanthropic interpretation, a way to bond couples throughout the year? Or, since no one knows just by looking at a pregnant lady which was the crucial coupling during the course of the month, is it just a way for perfidious women to keep men guessing who the father is?

Just recently a new, surprising theory has been proposed that cuts through – or at the very least modifies – all these arguments. Maybe, just like baboons, women don't have completely concealed ovulation at all.

Debra Lieberman admits that conversations can sometimes get a bit repetitive at parties, when her job comes up. "It always," she says, "comes round to disgust or incest."

Professor Lieberman, an evolutionary psychologist at the University of Miami, is interested in "kin detection" – the ability to identify relatives. The reason animals have kin detection systems is not because it's nice to spot your father and ask him how he is; it's because it's nice to spot your father and then be disgusted by the idea of having sex with him should the thought arise.

Incest is a very bad idea. It dramatically increases the chance of getting a genetic illness, as offspring are far likelier to get shared copies of a faulty gene. The extra genetic similarity between you and your child also makes it far more likely that all the harmful bacteria and viruses that like you will also like, and find a home in, them.

"For this reason," says Professor Lieberman, "you'd expect a kin detection system to be hooked into a mechanism such as the disgust response, that steers you away from relatives." The theory of evolution clearly predicts we should develop an aversion to inbreeding.

We know this is true in humans, and works on the basis of proximity in childhood. Siblings who grow up together feel disgust at the idea of being romantically involved. When adopted, genetically unrelated siblings grow up together they experience the same aversion.

Professor Lieberman had a thought. What if there were subconscious ways to see this effect at work? What if these natural responses became stronger at the point where they mattered most: the point when a woman is most likely to have a baby? Do women, in other words, steer clear of relatives during ovulation?

She didn't have the time or resources to observe women directly, even if she could think of an experiment that could do so in a natural way. But she realised she did not need to: the data had already been collected. It was sitting on their mobile phones.

So she and her colleagues convinced 48 women to tell them when they last menstruated, and to give them their phone bill. Then they went down the itemised calls and marked their fathers' and mothers' numbers. A pattern became clear.

At around the time the women were estimated to be

ovulating, their most fertile period, the number of calls to their fathers dropped. So too did the length of those calls they did make. This wasn't solely because they were focusing on romance rather than family, as there was no such change with their mums: something seemed to be warning them off interacting with their dads specifically.

Hidden in every woman's phone bill, if we had only known to look, is evidence of an inbreeding avoidance system.[62]

"Now no woman has the idea, 'I'm ovulating – see you later, Dad,'" says Lieberman, who stresses that her work still needs to be replicated – it was still a relatively small sample size. Neither, she adds, do they say, "I'm going to put on a sexy dress and head into town." Yet there is increasing evidence that, subconsciously, they do both those things – along with a whole suite of other behavioural changes linked to their increased fertility.

The behavioural changes are so subtle that until a decade or so ago they had mostly been missed. Any single investigation into them, such as the telephone calls study, could be dismissed as a fluke. Of all the areas of study in this book, these form the newest field of research – and the most likely to be challenged. Between writing this and the time of publication some may be overturned, others confirmed.

Slowly, though, the evidence has accumulated. Taken together, a diverse group of studies form a whole that, although composed of some pretty salacious factoids, has a certain gravity to it.

Studies find that when women are ovulating, they go out more, wear sexier clothes,[63] feel more attractive and – presumably because the risk of unwanted conception is higher – are more likely to rate men as potential rapists.[64] They spot the signs in other women as well – if they have an attractive partner they will try to keep ovulating women away from him.[65]

So large do some scientists believe the effects are that they have expressed concern about the pill. It works to suppress ovulation, meaning that when couples get together the woman's sexual psychology is significantly different from what it would be were she fertile. Then at just the point when the couple needs to be strongest – when they are planning for a baby – she comes off the pill and sees her partner with fertile eyes for the first time.*

Men notice too. They prefer the smell of a T-shirt worn by a woman who is fertile.[66] They are more protective of their partner when she is ovulating. According to one famous, and controversial, study lap dancers get bigger tips when they are most fertile.[67]

Just as with testosterone, here is something biological, playing out on the social stage, that is having clear effects on behaviour. And these are not even ovulation's most intriguing effects.

Lauren Lake's Paternity Court is not, it must be admitted, an official branch of the judiciary. Ms Lake does have a way with a gavel though, and according to Wikipedia is something of

---

* In a neat mirror of the telephone research, Sarah Hrdy, the prima-tologist, even hints that this might interfere with incest avoidance mechanisms. Ovulating women may prefer the scent of males with different immune attributes – presumably to keep them away from relatives. "Instead of preferring alien smells, very different from their own, however, women taking birth control pills that simulate preg-nancy exhibit the reverse preference."

a polymath, having worked as a "family lawyer, author, interior designer, real estate developer, [and] background singer". More pertinently, she offers paternity tests – the results of which are revealed after all parties involved have first exposed their most intimate secrets to her on daytime TV.

We join the exchange during a case one morning in 2017, via syndicated cable television, at the point at which the witness (Aisha Bryson, the mother of an 18-month old of disputed paternity) is being questioned about why her partner (Jamar McCarroll, the disputed father in question) felt the need to take her to this court.* He claims the child is not his, and he does not want to support it. She claims that it is his, and any suggestion to the contrary is just him projecting his own promiscuity onto her.

Or, as she puts it, addressing the "judge"…

Ms Bryson: "Mr McCarroll, he has whoreish ways. He wants me to be a whore like he is. And I'm just not that type of person."

Judge Lauren Lake: "Mr McCarroll, you want her to be a whore like you are?"

Mr McCarroll (who, according to the evidence presented, at the very least doesn't have monkish ways): "No, your honour, I have no idea where Ms Bryson gets that from."

To resolve the case, Ms Lake called on an extra witness – the competing potential father – before revealing the results of the DNA test. Which was the father? Neither of them.

That is actually such a common outcome in these shows it doesn't even classify as a twist.

---

* To be completely clear, while undoubtedly an august institution, *Lauren Lake's Paternity Court* does not yet have the legal power to subpoena witnesses. All parties volunteered for its services.

There are competitors. *Maury*, for instance, is a talk show that has a special paternity section. A tradition has developed there that when wouldn't-be fathers find themselves exonerated by a paternity test they stand up and do a little breakdance.

One regular guest on *Maury*, five dancing non-dads later, merited her own episode, titled: "I've tested five men...will I finally find my baby's dad?"

It is easy at this point to judge, to talk of societal breakdown – or even of an underclass. Perhaps for some there is even a temptation, guiltily suppressed, to use those words that have shamed promiscuous women down the centuries: slut, slag, whore. Resist.

Think instead of the conditions that led the women to behave in this way. I don't mean that in the way it is normally meant, where they are viewed, perhaps paternalistically, as victims of poverty, of ignorance or feckless men. Save your pity. Imagine, instead, that they are the ones with the agency – and that their response is an evolved one, precisely designed for the social circumstances in which they find themselves.

This was what Sarah Hrdy considered. "Nuclear families and exclusive partnerships devoted to child rearing are very much part of the human condition," she said. "But so – in some environments – are more casual unions...Under some economic circumstances, it just may not be feasible for one man to provide for a family – either because in his world successful hunting is unpredictable, or because in places like inner cities decent jobs are not available. Wherever fathers prove unreliable providers or protectors, it makes sense for mothers – if they are free to do so – to line up one or several 'secondary' fathers," and not put all their (literal) eggs in one monogamous basket. In other words, it may be sensible to have a lot of men who think they might be the father.

"In post-industrial countries, it is fashionable to assume that such arrangements are novel or 'unnatural' and to blame them on a 'breakdown' of the nuclear family brought about by feminism, or by the promiscuity resulting from an increase in the use of birth control." On the contrary, Hrdy argues, they are almost certainly a response that is part of the evolved human repertoire, "and likely to be far more ancient than either [feminism] or the pill".

So there is good reason for women, as at Lauren Lake's paternity court, to create confusion about the father – intentionally or not. That is just one of the strategies that concealed ovulation gives them. The other – subtly but importantly different – is not "disputed paternity" but "false paternity", that is, when a man is blithely and happily unaware that he is not the father. By its very nature, it is extremely difficult to study. Its prevalence is a question that biologists have puzzled over – with estimates in the past ranging from a few per cent to as high as a third of all babies. So how can we get closer to the truth, in a more systematic way than is offered even by *Maury*?

Genetic counselling is a new profession, but most big hospitals will have staff specialising in it. If a baby is born with a genetic disease, then a counsellor will analyse the parents' DNA to try to work out what was involved – and the chances of it affecting their next baby. So they are used to breaking difficult news.

However, there is one type of news that is so difficult to break that most counsellors admit they would deliberately deceive at least one of the parents or, according to one set of guidance, "fudge the issue".[68] This is despite the fact that most counsellors also expect this situation to present itself in their careers, probably several times.

Ostensibly it is good news: they have found the couple's *next* baby is very unlikely to have the feared condition. The reason why, though, is seriously awkward news: the real father of *this* baby with the genetic condition is not the man sitting in front of them. The genetic tests have shown that the woman's partner has been cuckolded. What do counsellors do in such circumstances? To not tell the father leaves him with the impression that he carries the genes for a genetic disease. To tell him is a direct, and potentially catastrophic, intervention in someone else's relationship.

As a messy compromise, a consensus is building that counsellors have a "frank discussion" with the woman – and leave what happens next in her hands.

If such chance discoveries, known as "inadvertent false paternity disclosure", are a dilemma for the medical profession, they are a boon for biologists. They provide a rare window onto women's sexuality and sexual strategies, unclouded by the one major biological weapon they have: their control of paternity.

Men have a significant advantage when it comes to sex. Biologically speaking, they need invest almost nothing in a baby – although it is very pertinent that culturally that is often not the case. Historically, it would have been extremely rare for a single mother to successfully raise a child without help either from a father or extended family. That is arguably why studies show women consistently find wealth makes men more attractive, but the reverse is not true.[69] This is also why most societies have found ways, whether through legal force or through the power of shame, to make unwilling father-hood costly. That is also why the non-dads on *Maury* danced.

But women have a biological advantage too. They, at least, are absolutely certain all their children are theirs. It is this that led to the "sexy sons hypothesis", the idea that women may look for one set of attributes in long-term partners, who can support their children, and another in short-term part-ners, whose genes they can sneakily acquire.

This is where some of the most interesting ovulation results come in. Two chapters ago, Gordon Gallup talked about some of the motivations for cheating – the idea that women might look for "dads" to look after their children, but have a motivation to seek out the better genes of "cads" for secret couplings. By looking at changes around ovulation, we can see both evidence and a mechanism for just this.

The results remain controversial, but several studies have found that during ovulation women shift in their preferences. When they are ovulating they seem to be less interested in the kind of reliable man who could pay the mortgage, and more interested in the sort of man who would turn up on a Harley and whisk them away to Vegas, before losing the mortgage on the craps table. It is not necessarily correct to say that their priorities change; they may still say that they want a man who will stick around. It's just that during ovulation they have a different understanding of who that would be.

Or, as Kristina Durante writes in a 2012 paper that inves-tigated just this,[70] fertile women are more likely to believe "that charismatic and adventurous cads will become more-investing fathers and more committed and stable romantic partners, at least with respect to them." The last clause is key. They still know in their heart of hearts that the man putting on the leather jacket and showing off his pool skills in the bar isn't going to be the most stable choice – when asked whether he would stick around in a relationship with a different partner who wasn't them, their opinion was closer to reality. What the researchers found was that the ovulating women "believe that a charismatic and adventurous cad will be a better father if he conceives a child with them, but not with other women," wrote Professor Durante, from the University of Texas, San Antonio.

The consequences are clear. During ovulation, "When presented with a romantic offer from a sexy cad, the hormonal changes associated with fertility can lead Mr. Wrong to appear like Mr. Right."

Why would this be? Professor Durante has her theories. One idea is that getting a nice smouldering alpha male is just too good a proposition to pass up. "Perceiving sexy cads as good dads is ultimately more of a short-term sexual strategy geared toward securing genetic benefits with an occasional long-term payoff. Missing a mating opportunity with such men would have been more costly for these women at high fertility. After all, you never know; you could be 'the one'."

Even if he isn't in the mood for settling, a covert liaison with the cad, while keeping the dad unaware, is a good plan B. This may be why women seem to also be more interested in short-term relationships when ovulating. It could also be why those in relationships they are unhappy with are more likely to avoid their boyfriend's calls at that time.[71]

For her part, Professor Lieberman thinks it is not so binary, or calculating. She thinks that women's priorities subtly shift on a continuum, encouraging different compromises, but that the ultimate Prince Charming ideal remains unchanged.

"It's taken as an assumption, I don't know if it should be, that women have long-term and short-term mating strategies," she says. "Not all beefcake men are cads, not all sensible-looking men are dads."

So it is perfectly possible to seek both. "I don't think women necessarily have a short-term mating strategy. Instead, they have adaptations that assess their own 'leverage' in the mating game and when their leverage is high – when they are fertile – they go for broke: get the sexy guy and have him fall in love with you *and only you*. When this strategy fails, it looks like a short-term mating strategy. I really think what ends up becoming a short-term relationship is a failed bet – a failed risky bet."

One morning, in 18th-century Italy, Lazzaro Spallanzani decided to dress some frogs. At the time, science was pretty vague about what it was that a man brought to the process of reproduction. People had already seen sperm under a microscope, but there was no consensus about what it did. Was it actually, as had been presumed periodically by different civilisations throughout history, "seed"?

Spallanzani wanted to find out – so he found some frogs and, at mating time, put them in trousers.

To his surprise they seemed happy enough with the arrangement. "The males, notwithstanding this encumbrance, seek the females with equal eagerness, and perform, as well as they can, the act of generation," he wrote.

He conceded the "breeches" might seem "whimsical and ridiculous", but their purpose was not sartorial. They were there to act as a barrier – a frog condom. The frogs could still mate but the trousers meant, in his words, that the "eggs are never prolific, for want of having been bedewed with semen, which sometimes may be seen on the breeches in the form of drops". He then collected some of those bedewed drops, added them to eggs, and made some tadpoles.[72,] *

If we were uncertain for a long time what sperm did, it took even longer to work out eggs.

In 1951 Pope Pius XII gave a speech based on cutting-edge science. He stated that "the will [of a marital couple] to avoid the fecundity of their union, while continuing to satisfy to the full their sensuality, can only be the result of

---

* This may not have been the first artificial insemination. There were persistent rumours that in 1461 Henry IV of Castile, after failing to produce an heir, tried it out successfully on his wife Joan. That said, the *noms de guerre* given to that line of royals tell their own story. While Henry II gained the – for a medieval king – relatively honourable appellation "the fratricidal", Henry IV was called "the impotent" – and his daughter, the supposed product of this artificial insemination, simply "the bastard". The first verifiable human artificial insemination was several centuries later, by the surgical pioneer John Hunter. He also goes down as one of the most enthusiastic investigators of human reproduction ever, with experiments into semen composition that are still rarely repeated (in a scientific context, at least). "The smell of semen is mawkish and unpleasant," he wrote in 1786, "exactly resembling a Spanish chestnut; and, to the taste, though at first insipid, it has so much pungency as after some little time to stimulate and excite a degree of heat in the mouth". He also noted that the "first part of the emission is evidently different from the last", a statement that would dangle tantalisingly in the scientific literature for two centuries before being followed up by a handful of sperm scientists, who claimed to have discovered there really are differences in human ejaculate composition – with some spurts containing "killer sperm", designed to attack that of rivals. Alas, subsequent investigation, in which unrelated sperm was put in a petri dish and left to fight it out, did not seem to back up their claims.

a false appreciation of life and of motives foreign to sound ethical principles", but that in certain "grave circumstances" the "observance of the natural sterile periods may be lawful, from the moral viewpoint". He had just given (very) qualified approval to the "rhythm method" – the idea that having sex at certain times of the month and avoiding it at others could be a means of contraception.

That this was possible had incredibly only been fully appreciated a little over 20 years earlier, when scientists worked out how – and when – eggs made their journey from the ovary. Until that time, some had thought the fertile window was around menstruation, others that there wasn't one – and women could become pregnant at any time in the cycle.*

So it is not surprising that pre-scientific societies in the remoter parts of the world still cling onto eclectic ideas regarding how reproduction occurs.

Anthropologists have found some tribes who believe semen has to mix with menstrual blood to be effective. Others believe that foetuses require semen to grow, and so having sex with several men before and during pregnancy ensures a healthier baby. Still others, in the Amazon, believe in "partible paternity" – formalising this process of multiple fathers with a hierarchy of "primary" and "secondary" fathers

---

* The rhythm method offers an extreme parable of why human reproduction is so strange – and why scientists have been so keen to work out why women don't visibly and clearly advertise their fertility. By having sex throughout the month, even when it is probably pointless, couples "waste" energy. More than that, though, because sperm can hang around in the woman's body, they run the risk of old sperm fertilising an egg, leading to birth defects. That means that those engaging in the rhythm method are using not only a highly ineffective contraceptive, but, also, according to some scientists, one that makes the unwanted pregnancies that result more likely to go wrong.

– just the arrangement that Professor Hrdy suggested women might choose in difficult environments. These societies have, in effect, institutionalised both paternity uncertainty and promiscuity. This is insurance against choosing a husband who turns out to be infertile – and as a bonus afterwards ensures fatherly support from more than one man. Children in this society who benefit from more than one supposed father have been found to be more likely to survive.

It also speaks to another theory that offers a wholly different explanation for female promiscuity and concealed ovulation – and for women behaving differently at the crucial point when they are ovulating.

Think back to the woman on *Maury*, with her five potential dads (none of whom were actually the dad). In the west, that level of promiscuity is often seen as shameful – appearing in public to talk about it more shameful still. Professor Hrdy suggested one explanation why it is actually a sensible strategy – as a means of getting help from a selection of men.

She offered another explanation too, based on an experience that, she said, was the only time she had ever cried while out on fieldwork.

In 1972, early in her career, she was observing a troop of langurs on Mount Abu, in Rajasthan. A new alpha male, called Mug, had just taken control of a harem – one of the females of which was still nursing her infant, Scratch.

Over the days following his takeover, Professor Hrdy watched Mug become more aggressive towards Scratch. "While looking everywhere but at the true focus of his attention, Mug would edge ever closer to his object, the infant Scratch. Every movement the male made, even innocent foraging, was a potential feint. The females were exhausted from having to stay ahead of him. The double duty of avoiding the male and staying fed was taking its toll." Eventually the inevitable happened.

"Mug wrested Scratch from his mother and ran off with the infant in his mouth. Once again, the two older females, Sol and Pawless, charged the male to wrest the infant from him. Before they succeeded the infant was bitten in the skull and received a gash on his thigh and lower abdomen so deep that the intestines could be seen within."

The idea the professor suggests is that, while it may be bad, evolutionarily speaking, to mate indiscriminately and not be selective with partners, it is even worse to have an offspring that gets killed, as happened to Scratch's mother.

Mug's was a sensible, if gruesome, strategy – and it is something that happens in many mammal societies. When a new male takes over, he kills any nursing offspring – mothers who are breastfeeding are unlikely to get pregnant. So, to protect their offspring, mothers need their own strategy: what if the male thinks there is a chance that the existing offspring are his? Then, killing a baby suddenly becomes a very bad strategy indeed. Had Mug been uncertain on this point, then perhaps Scratch's fate would have been different. So what if females had sex with lots of males?

The idea, translating this into humans, is that having a fair bit of how's your father also creates a fair bit of "Who's your father?" – and that can be protective.

Only recently have we had the ability to really assess paternity confusion on a population level. Before widespread genetic testing there were glimpses. There is a classic piece of research from the 1970s – known as the "Liverpool flats study" – in which the residents of a whole block of flats were blood-typed, in which process it was inadvertently revealed that 20-30 per cent of the block's children were not fathered by the man they called Dad.

At the time, it was dismissed as irrelevant on the grounds that you could expect little else from Liverpudlians. Later, it was dismissed on the arguably even more solid grounds that while lots of people have referred to it, no one has actually seen the original research – or even definitively knows who did it.[73]

As better data has come in, including from some clever studies that compared genetic testing to genealogies to look back several centuries, a consensus has developed that the true figure is probably around a tenth of that – which is still pretty high, by most people's standards. Whether or not that Liverpudlian apartment block ever existed, it was not representative, at least, of post-agricultural societies – small-scale research in hunter-gatherer societies has found similar levels, with up to a third of men being cuckolded.[74]

Even so, and even with contraception freely available, the conclusion is clear. In the average-sized primary-school classroom there will be a child who is unaware who his or her real father is. In the average commuter train carriage, where perhaps you are reading this, there will be several adults still unaware. There is one development that means for the next generation it could be even higher: the internet.

It was a strange feeling, to be judged as morally suspect by a group of people who had gathered together with the express intention of having affairs. But there was no question, even so, that I was being judged. "You look too young to be disillusioned with your marriage," said one woman. "How long have you been married?" Three years, I replied. "You should be in the honeymoon period." She disapproved. "Why are you doing this?" She lifted her mask up to take a drink, and surveyed the room for a more respectable philanderer.

The real answer was, I had been sent by the newspaper for which I work, *The Times*, to report on a masked ball for people seeking extramarital affairs. But the UK website behind it, called Illicit Encounters, had only allowed me entry on condition that I did not reveal my true identity. Just four of its clients were told who I really was, and were preselected for me to interview.

One was Suzy, 38, there with her sister. Sitting on a sofa, she said that as she reached her late thirties she realised she just needed something else, that she had, "been a mum and wife for years. Now it's got to the point where my home life isn't enough. I love my husband, and I love my life with my husband. I know it sounds weird, but I just want more".

Doubtless many people in marriages far into their second decade want more, but until recently achieving it was a risky process. It involved deception, the fear of discovery and – even if you decided to go ahead – the not insignificant difficulty of finding someone to have an affair with.

Humans are designed to watch out for cheating. The existence of jealousy as a powerful emotion is proof of that. For women, a cheating partner is bad news primarily because it means their relationship might break down. For men that is also a grave concern but, from an evolutionary perspective, there is an even worse outcome to having an unfaithful partner – that they might end up unwittingly looking after a child that is not their own.

So it is not at all surprising that in the modern world men who even suspect they have been cuckolded will reduce the time they spend with the child, and take less interest in his or her education.[75] It is also not surprising that the sex with the most to lose will be more suspicious. When asked how likely it is that their partner will cheat on them, men consistently give a higher probability than women. To be fair, if men are pessimistic about their wives' faithfulness, they feel the same way about their own. They are also more likely than women to say that they will cheat.[76]

And who should men and women be suspicious of? Research has found that when men pass a selection of rival males they pay most attention to those who are high status. Women, on the other hand, pay more attention to rivals who are attractive[77] (even to the extent that they are more likely to remember their locations afterwards, all the better, presumably, to keep their menfolk away).[78]

The internet, superficially at least, has made finding a willing extramarital partner far easier – and the chance of discovery far smaller. Suzy didn't need to risk flirting at the tennis club, or approaching men in bars – where she might be noticed by friends, or rejected and embarrassed. All she needed to do to get the "more" she was looking for was go online and find a dating site specifically for people like her. Illicit Encounters was perfect because, she said, the risk was gone – or, rather, precisely offset. "If he found out, it would be a devastation." Online, the only person who can reveal you (excluding hackers) is the other person who also does not want to be found out. "The whole benefit of this site is both parties have too much to lose." In terms of revealing the affair, it is mutually assured destruction.

After speaking, we returned to the party, where an intricate ice-breaking game was underway. Each woman had a necklace with a padlock. Each man had a key, which would only fit one padlock. It was like Cinderella's slipper, but with significantly more conversational double entendres along the lines of "why don't you put your key in my lock and give it a good jiggle?"

By the time last orders approached the masks had gone, and my cover story was blown. After several hours of drinking, the event had become less *Eyes Wide Shut*, more predatory hen party. "This is Tom from *The Times*, I've been telling you about him," said one of my earlier interviewees, dragging me towards her friends. "Ooh, he's nice," said one. "Do you have affairs, Tom? Are you married?" I stuttered. Then a 40-something in a feather boa saved me. "No, he's gay," she said. "I can tell. You're gay, aren't you, Tom?"

I fled, escaping the feather boa, for the youth, vitality and optimism of the street below.

But coming out of the doorway, in the light drizzle of a London evening, I ran straight into Suzy and her sister, both in a clench with rotund bankers. Suzy looked briefly at me, peering over her conquest's shoulder. Then, with a moue, she turned away and lunged in for a snog.

5

ZEUS

A king's legacy is a queen's burden

And He took him outside and said, "Now look toward the heavens, and count the stars, if you are able to count them." And He said to him, "So shall your descendants be."

Genesis 15:5

The boys descended like a plague. Without warning they arrived, a ravaging horde of adolescents and "little tyrants". Rampaging through the streets of 18th-century Meknes, then the capital of Morocco, they would go from market stall to market stall, taking whatever they wanted.

"When they appear in the city, every man hides all that they may happen to fancy, for they lay hold of everything greedily, they rob without fear of punishment," wrote one appalled western visitor. No one was spared from the attention of these children: "They have been seen to snatch the very bread out of the mouths of slaves."

All they could do was wait for the swarm to pass – and prepare for the next one which, the shopkeepers knew, would be even worse and even larger. "No man dares touch them," the same visitor said, "as they grow up [they] increase in malice and rob, abuse and kill."

The reason the boys had such licence was that they were the sons of the king of Morocco. And the reason they were such a menace was that there were 600 of them, and their numbers were still growing.

The problem with much research into sexuality is that it can only go so far. This is because understandably we don't, generally, get to perform experiments on humans – at least not ones that intervene in their actual procreation. So we can, for instance, look at people's reactions to being propositioned on the street, but not take that proposition through to its logical conclusion. We can look at fruit fly sex, but not human sex.

But there are two men, utterly untroubled by the evolutionary theory of sex differences, who have inadvertently provided material for two of the most powerful investigations into it – offering natural experiments into the limits of reproduction. Through them, theory meets reality, albeit an extreme version of reality.

Their example provides some of the most compelling arguments in support of much of what has been written in this book so far. These men come from two very different times and places. Both were powerful. Both greatly increased the world's misery – one in how he lived, the other in how he died.

The second was just a joker who couldn't see when the joke had gone too far. He would have been appalled by the wretchedness he caused. The first? Well, Sultan Moulay Ismael the

Bloodthirsty was not given to introspection. Particularly when he was wearing yellow.

Even at the best of times, the Moroccan ruler could be capricious. "It is one of his common diversions, at one motion, to mount his horse, draw his scimitar, and cut off the head of the slave who holds his stirrups," wrote Dominique Busnot, a French friar who had come to his court in the hope of freeing some of those slaves – preferably with their heads still in place.

Several times a day the sultan changed his clothes, and with them his mood. And when, wrote Busnot, he emerged wearing yellow, "all men quake and avoid his presence; for that is the colour he puts on when he designs some bloody execution". Gone was the playful skittishness of horsey beheadings. In was serious, focused murder.

This was when he would, say, order his woodcutters to saw a man in half, lengthways – angled more towards the crotch than the head, so it lasted longer. Or he would sit traitors on iron spikes so that they slowly died over three days. Perhaps instead he might do a spot of redecorating – nailing some Moors to the city gates or stringing the ears of his defeated foes on chains over the streets as grisly bunting.*

In 18th-century North Africa it took quite some effort to so distinguish yourself in mindless violence, against a background noise of pretty constant mindless violence, that you gained the honorific "The Bloodthirsty" – but he more than earned it.

---

* Animals were not spared either. Once, when a cat displeased him, he ordered an executioner to drag it through the streets, scourge it severely, behead it and cry throughout "with a loud voice…'Thus my master uses knavish cats'".

Which makes it all the more notable that today he is best known for making love, not war. Dominique Busnot's account of the court of Moulay Ismael the Bloodthirsty has become one of the more significant, and unlikely, citations in modern sex research, because of his description of Moulay Ismael's sex life.

Moulay Ismael's harem was legendary. At any one time he kept 500 concubines. They lived with him until the age of 30, locked in the gilded cage of his palace – a vast complex in Meknes, the construction of which continued all his life.

One of the only accounts we have of the inner sanctum is from a Dutch slave girl, who described the sultan sitting in splendour with 50 of his women as "they played and sang…a melody more lovely than anything I'd ever heard before".

For variety he did occasionally take them on supervised trips to inspect the construction progress of the palace: he travelling by chariot, they pulling it. Then when they grew too old, they were moved along with any children they had to live out their days in a different palace, a retirement home for concubines.

This happy arrangement enabled Moulay Ismael to have a constant supply of nubile attendants, right until the end of his days. Quite literally. On his deathbed, it was said by one of those present that he ordered his concubines to his room and "demanded such disgusting acts that decency won't allow us to relate them".

The arrangement also enabled him to enter the record books, through an experiment on the limits of male fertility. Because not only did Moulay Ismael never want for a fertile, non-pregnant woman, he also seemed to always have the appetite for one – as evidenced by his demands even while dying.

If the sultan had 600 sons, basic probability implies he also had just under 600 daughters – on average 1.05 boys are born for every girl. Unfortunately this can't be confirmed by counting the princesses: according to Busnot all girl babies except those born to his four official wives were strangled at birth. But there are clues elsewhere this estimate might not be far off the mark. Whenever the sultan had a child, boy or girl, he raised a tax on the Jews to pay for gifts. The records show at least 1,200 such levies.

This implies two things. First, he celebrated babies even while ordering their strangulation – institutional antisemitism was evidently a pastime as well as a duty. Second, Moulay Ismael is probably the most fecund man in history.

Of course, no one can know for sure that another man has not exceeded his record. Maybe Genghis Khan had more children. Maybe some recent Saudi royal does. Perhaps instead the accolade goes to an anonymous Scandinavian sperm donor – it is a happy state of human affairs that the genes now being selected as most reproductively successful are those that produce not murderous tyrants but men willing to have a philanthropic weekly contemplation in a cubicle.

Crucially, Moulay's tally aligns with theory. In 2014 a paper was published in the scientific press, titled "The Case of Moulay Ismael – Fact or Fancy?"[79] It posed the question: over a 30-year period, how many copulations per day would have been necessary for him to reach his total? The Austrian scientists calculated that with a relatively restrained one to two acts of random fornication per day he could have easily romped home, so to speak. For a ruler who, while dying, still required his concubines to perform acts that caused chroniclers to blush, this is surely an unremarkable feat.

If 1,200 children represents, approximately, the upper limit of male reproduction, what is the figure for females? That number, tellingly, is found by looking not at the richest and most powerful people in the world – but at those at the bottom of society.

The Great Stork Derby began in Toronto just before the Great Depression with the death of Charles Vance Millar and the reading of his will. "This Will is necessarily uncommon and capricious," it began. "I have no dependants or near relations and no duty rests upon me to leave any property at my death and what I do leave is proof of my folly in gathering and retaining more than I required in my lifetime."

As it turned out, his folly had been great. Millar's fortune after death was considerable – perhaps £5-10m in today's money – and growing, thanks to prudent investments that matured soon after.

From his will, it is possible to infer something of Vance Millar's character. A Toronto businessman, he clearly disliked the streak of prohibition-era puritanism currently prevalent even north of the US border, that took it upon itself to pruriently limit others' vices, whether gambling, sex or drinking. So he decided to expose it as hypocrisy – or at least give people some good laughs trying.

"To each duly ordained Minister of a Christian Church resident at my death in Towns of Walkerville and Sandwich and the City of Windsor and earning an annual salary expounding the scripture to the sinners there," he wrote, "I give one share of the Kenilworth Jockey Club."

Having given one group of priests a stake in a gambling den, he then gave some Protestant ministers a share in a brewery. The joke, much enjoyed by the public, was compounded when some actually applied for the shares, and found they were valued at half a cent.

The joke that had the longest life, though, even if by the end few found it funny, was clause 9. He instructed that his executors hold his remaining assets for ten years and give them "to the mother who has since my death given birth in Toronto to the greatest number of children".

In just a few short sentences, he set in motion a competition that would occupy the press of Toronto and beyond for a decade – and then at the end of that decade, with a several-way tie, provide much useful employment for the city's lawyers.

But what would be known in the press as the Great Stork Derby was far more than a quirky diversion. For newspapers, this was a bounty the like of which is rarely seen – a grand human drama, guaranteed to persist for a decade, that was essentially all about sex. It was also the biggest natural experiment ever into the limits of female fertility.

With the Derby barely a month old, the *Toronto Daily Star* had already declared five mothers of twins to be in an early lead. Four years in, they had assigned a permanent reporter on the story, had informants in maternity hospitals and would approach pregnant women in the street to buy up picture and interview rights.

For Millar's relatives, who had presumed they would become wealthy on his death, the Derby was less entertaining. Their line of attack, in questioning the will, focused on morality. The contest offered women – married or unmarried – an incentive "to compete against each other in sexual indulgence".

The cases were dismissed. In the end the only moral statement in court that really seemed sincere came after the event. Justice Middleton, the judge who ruled on the final validity of the will, added an aside in his judgment, "I would regard the clause in question as prompted rather by sympathy for the mothers of large families, who are often extremely poor people, not unmingled by a grim sense of humour...As to the effect of such a gift, the testator's attitude seems to me rather like the throwing of a handful of coins for the pleasure of seeing children scramble for it."

Because despite the initial frivolity of what Millar had started, three years later as the economy crashed, the grim reality could not be avoided. Most of those competing for his pot of cash were living on food stamps. They had been offered the chance of unimaginable wealth, but to achieve it had to support a large and growing family – in the knowledge that if they came second they would have nothing. It would be difficult to devise a contest more likely to promote human misery.

As each year came and went, the newspapers all over North America produced leader tables of the top performing women. Like the football leagues, where teams are ordered by points but the position is also tempered by games played, they would note in brackets whether the woman was also pregnant at the time. Then the next year would come and you would see whether she had miscarried.

Other tables showed previous form as well, citing not just the babies eligible to be counted but those born before. As the final lap approached Grace Bagnato, for instance, had an impressive 23 in the "Born" column of the *New York Times'* table – of whom nine were eligible.

More stark, though, was another number, put in parentheses: surviving children. She had just 14 of those.

Afterwards, a journalist reflected on that time in his career. "Looking back, the things I remember most are the smell of many children in bad houses; the unnatural talk about big money by tired women living on relief; the resigned resentment of husbands whose procreative powers had suddenly become world news."

Following deductions for stillborns, and legal wrangling over illegitimate births, the final result was a tie: four mothers on nine births each.

By that time, many of the leading contenders had already planned how to spend their money. One wanted an education for all her children, one a new car, another to build a row of cheap homes for the poor. One wanted a divorce. Grace Bagnato said, "All I want is quiet." Lucy Timleck, who had 16 surviving children in total, half born before the contest began, said she wanted to fund a job as an advocate of birth control.

Legal arguments aside, the competition had lasted for ten years. Extrapolated over the course of 30 fertile years for each woman, the findings of the derby were that the upper limit for female fecundity is around 30 offspring in a lifetime.

Historical evidence implies this is not too far from the truth. In 1989, for instance, one Maria Benita Olivera from Argentina ended an astonishing run of reproduction – having kicked off her fertile life with triplets at the age of 13, she called her childbearing years to a halt at the age of 49 with a single birth, and the words "I can't have any more. One more and I'm dead." She is tied on 32 babies with at least three other women around the world.*

The conclusions are clear. In his lifetime, given the means and opportunity, a man can easily sire more than a thousand babies. A woman can manage a 40th of that figure – but do so in what are likely to be fairly uncomfortable, if not life-threatening, circumstances.

For the man, the minimum investment in each of those children is a swift visit to the harem between restorative slave beheadings. For the woman, it is nine months – nine months in which she is vulnerable, sick and has to source better-quality food while also finding it harder to move. At the end of those nine months, she has to risk her own and her baby's life in what is still the most dangerous undertaking most healthy adult women will routinely endure: childbirth. Then, she will need to raise the baby, all the while eating enough to support breastfeeding. She also needs to wean each baby at a stage in its development when it is extremely vulnerable.

---

* According to *The Guinness Book of Records* the most fertile woman in history is the wife of 18th-century Russian peasant Feodor Vassilyev. Her parish records, which found their way into the medical journal *The Lancet*, describe 69 births; 16 twins, seven triplets and four quads. It was, *The Lancet* said with certain scepticism, a case of "quite extraordinary fecundity" – but the journal added that it seemed to be true: in 1872, it claimed, most of the offspring were still alive.

"This fact, almost incredible, is stated to be, nevertheless authentic. M. Khanikoff, correspondent of the Imperial Academy of St. Petersburg, was consulted a few years ago...He replied that all investigation was superfluous, that the family in question still lived in Moscow and had received favours from the Government."

Now without wishing to impugn the honour of the estimable M. Khanikoff, it is worth noting that if indeed correct this would also add astonishing longevity to fertility – most of those 69 children would have been centenarians by then.

The only clear reproductive advantage she does have in this transaction is that, unlike the man, she can be absolutely certain that the baby is hers. When Moulay Ismael went for a turn in the gardens with his concubines, it wasn't solely for recreation that he got his eunuchs to fan out in front of him like beaters, shooting any man who looked in his harem's direction.

In the right circumstance a man can make 1,200 children, with relative ease. A woman can make 30, with an almost superhuman effort. Moulay Ismael had people to look after each of his babies, whereas the mothers in the Great Stork Derby had to shoulder the burden themselves (at best sharing the load with the fathers). If you want to understand the difference between how males and females approach sex, then these are the two numbers that matter. Because, bluntly, if male and female sexual behaviours have not evolved to exploit that difference then evolution does not work.

There is a question at the heart of any book like this. It is, are the patterns of sexual behaviour we see a reflection of nature, or nurture? Are they caused by genes, or environment? The first answer is, they are by necessity about both.

The patriarchy is often invoked as the true cause of apparent sex differences. The patriarchy is real, and it really causes – or at the very least exaggerates – some differences in male and female sexuality. It ensures women feel shame for promiscuity, while men get plaudits.

So that is an environmental cause. But the patriarchy itself is partly created by physical male strength. So that is a genetic cause. So is it nature or nurture? The question makes no sense. It must be both.

The second response, when people ask what causes today's sexual mores, is, even the bits of the question that do make sense are never fully answerable. We cannot run experiments on entire human cultures, running different versions of history to see if, say, you can create a polyamorous society by putting people in a place with more tempting fruit. Ultimately, we will never definitively adjudicate between the two. Both must be true.

This makes talking definitively about innate sex differences hard. I don't know for certain if men are innately more likely, say, to strive to be CEO of a hedge fund. I can't say whether women really do excel at multi-tasking. The further removed you are from sex, the harder the inference. Similarly I don't know exactly what testosterone does in humans – although I do know its effects don't end at hairiness.

But here's the thing. If you explained to an alien the rules of evolution, if you told them how *Homo sapiens* reproduced, and maybe showed them what happened in other animals, then the dynamic they would predict is probably the dynamic we have: men on average keener for sex, women on average pickier.

At some point, isn't it simplest just to assume that evolution is the reason why?

And yet, humans *are* different. Animals don't have culture,* or contraception. Theories of parental investment and differential sexual success might work for other species; they might even work for historical studies of humans, but, after sexual

---

* Or, at least, not much of it – without wishing to impugn tool-using dolphins.

revolutions and technological tumult, can we really still apply them to today's generations? Does Trivers prevail in a world of Tinder? In 2016, some scientists attempted to answer just that question, in a modern twist on the "Would you go to bed with me" experiment.

Even by the standards of the New York dating market, Hannah's was a bold gambit. One day, the 24-year-old declared herself open to offers from everyone within 100 miles.

You could be male, female, attractive, ugly, old, young. Your dating profile picture could be of a dark handsome stranger, or of a man with a swastika tattoo holding a placard promising to send pictures of his genitals. It didn't matter; Hannah was game.

The matches, and messages, started coming in immediately. Thousands of keen New Yorkers liked the look of Hannah. In fact, 10 per cent of the app's eligible New York users quickly indicated they would like a date with her.

Elsewhere in the city, another 24-year-old called Michael was employing the same strategy. Like Hannah he was averagely attractive, but he was doing less well. He liked just as many people, but just 0.6 per cent liked him back. Of those who did, subsequent analysis showed almost 90 per cent were gay men. Michael did not get many dates.

Which is fine, because Michael and Hannah didn't really exist. They are two of the many bots that roam the dating app Tinder, automated fishing programmes looking to reel people in for their own ulterior motives. The difference is, in this case the ulterior motive was not profit but dating research, and the creator was Gareth Tyson – a computer scientist whose own time on Tinder has not been, he admits, completely dissimilar from Michael's.

"Let's just say my experience maps into the empirical data," he says. "Sadly."

Researchers are only just beginning to make sense of the data produced by the world's online search for love. Where just a decade ago social scientists would write entire academic papers on the basis of a single speed-dating study involving a few dozen participants, today it is routine to analyse several million interactions between hundreds of thousands of singles, none of whom know that they are even involved in an experiment.

The results are surprising for just how unsurprising they are. As one data scientist put it, "You get the hardest-core clichés you could imagine…people are very stereotypical in aggregate."

So we find that the most popular women are thin, young and educated but not too educated. The most popular man is wealthy, with a doctorate (although not one he brags about) and looking for a relationship rather than casual sex.[80] In other words he is, in parental investment terms, a provider. Men market themselves by talking about their profession. Women market themselves by talking about their bodies.[81] Women lie about their weight, men lie about their height.[82]

Men are more attracted to screen names relating to appearance (for example Cutie, Blondie) – they are looking for fertility. Women are more attracted to screen names indicating intelligence (for example Cultured).[83] They are looking for resources. Women are happy (or at least happier) to consider older men, but they draw the line at shorter ones – refusing to look at the profiles of men they would look down on in heels. A subset of older women – shy cougars, if you will – browse the profiles of younger men but never muster the courage to message them.[84]

At all ages, the average woman's ideal man is roughly the same age as her. At all ages, the average man's ideal woman is aged 22. As men get older, the age range they consider having sex with widens. As women get older, it stays narrow.[85] The biggest predictor of whether a man gets a second date is if he is good at conversation, and appears interested in the woman. The biggest predictor of whether a woman gets a second date is what she looks like.

Dr Tyson, from Queen Mary University of London, wanted to see what he could add to this dataset, by looking at one of the newest, and biggest, apps of all: Tinder. Tinder users don't bother with carefully curated lists of their hobbies or qualifications. They don't specify whether they are looking for love or for sex. They don't eliminate anyone without GSOH.

Theirs is the simplest interaction conceivable. They browse a selection of photographs of people in the same area, choosing the ones they find attractive. If any of those people also find them attractive, they get to talk to them.

This makes it like old-fashioned dating in a bar or night-club – but at a frenetic pace. "The thing about Tinder that is interesting is the physical constraints are gone," says Dr Tyson. "You can only speak to five people in a nightclub – on Tinder you can speak to a hundred in a night."

That was why his Hannahs – Hannah was on the prowl in other parts of the world too, always called Hannah – made such a splash when they arrived on the Tinder scene. With no physical limitations, they could digitally "meet" hundreds of thousands of men. "Our female profiles were popular, really popular. Within seconds you get the first match." And the male profiles? "The number of matches is very, very, very slow."

It gets worse, for the Michaels. Dr Tyson has a theory that using apps like Tinder creates a spiral of male despair. Women's initial successes encourage them to be pickier – if everyone they choose also chooses them, they can have high standards. For men it is the reverse. Their initial failures eventually convince them the only strategy is to remove all standards.[86]

"Imagine if you're a woman. You create a profile, like somebody and immediately get a match. You learn very quickly you should only 'like' people you want. This polarises women to be very selective. Men are the opposite. They click like, get no matches – and get frustrated big time. So what guys try to do is match with everybody, and leave it for the women to decide."

Women get to be choosy, men get to be grateful. Was Dr Tyson surprised? "The study was proving the obvious; I wasn't surprised at all."

Maybe the women were right to be choosy. After the results were in, Dr Tyson conducted a survey. He asked people what they wanted from a match. Half of men said one of the most important uses of Tinder for them was to get one-night stands. Just 15 per cent of women felt the same way.

Until recently, there would have been a major counter-example to this: Ashley Madison. The very existence of the website which, like Illicit Encounters in the UK, allowed people to meet for extramarital affairs, seemed a rebuke to the idea that men and women were so fundamentally different. After all, for it to work at all there had to be people on both sides of the transaction.

Then on July 15, 2015, a group of hackers calling themselves the "Impact Team" announced they had stolen all its membership data – 35 million records were about to be released.

Some commentators prophesied a social catastrophe. What happens when, in one day, 35 million cheating spouses are exposed? All were agreed it was a disaster for Ashley Madison. Surely nothing could be worse PR for a site for people seeking extramarital affairs than for everyone involved to be exposed?

That's exactly what Ashley Madison wanted you to think. Because there is one outcome for an adultery service that is, incredibly, even worse PR. It is having everyone involved exposed, and then finding out that they are mostly men. Ashley Madison's business model involved charging men to use their services. Women used them for free. The hope was that this would achieve parity between the sexes. The raw data showed they were not even close.

30 million of those registered were male, just five million female. Then people started looking into activity on the site. Annalee Newitz, an editor at the website Gizmodo trawled through the hacked material, which included the website's source code.[87] She found that, much of the time, the women who messaged men weren't women at all. Like Hannah and Michael, the Tinder profiles who swiped right on the single population of entire cities, they existed only as code. These computer fictions were there to chat to the men on Ashley Madison, to keep them paying and engaged.

So the Tinder and Ashley Madison community, it seems, is a tragedy of mismatched expectations – of choosy versus indiscriminate, casual versus serious. The fault, though, is surely less in the app than in the participants. The fault is human beings.

Here is Trivers in the 21st century – ancient, evolved preferences, manifesting themselves on a touchscreen gps-enabled social networking app. Men look for quick gratification, compete hard for it and normally fail. Women look for long-term partners, have the pick of the suitors and still… normally fail. Is that, then, human sexuality explained? Here we have a theory, data to support the theory – and everything, surely, fits into place?

Almost everything.

If, instead of swiping left several hundred thousand times, Hannah and Michael had gone to the settings section of their profile, they would have noticed something that would have baffled Darwin, that would have left Bateman pretty confused, and which points to a far more complex world of human sexuality.

Click on the option "gender", and you are presented with 37 possibilities: from "androgyne" to "two-spirit". In between there is pansexual, homosexual, asexual and transsexual.

To begin to understand this confusing new world, you could embroil yourself in modern gender politics, you could acquaint yourself with the literature on the use of correct pronouns.

Or, you could just start by looking at penguins.

6

ACHILLES

The fatal flaw, and the love between men

There seems to be no crime too low for these penguins.
                                        George Levick, 1915

Joachim Schoene wants to be clear about one thing. He makes no judgment on the life choices of his penguins. "We're very happy about our gay couples," he says, earnestly. Schoene, one of the staff at Bremerhaven Zoo in Germany, is a northern European liberal, and he would never seek to make hetero-normative presumptions about the nature of a penguin's love life. That said, the Humboldt penguin is an endangered species. So while individually each bird in his care is absolutely empowered to decide its own path, conservation-wise it makes things a little tricky that so many choose to nest with a partner of the same sex.

It is not easy to sex a Humboldt penguin. So it was only when Bremerhaven Zoo decided to perform a DNA test on all of its flock that it found out the reason they were not reproducing so well. Six of them were in homosexual relationships.

The word "relationship", for penguins, is not too anthropomorphic – they really do form couples. The Bremerhaven enclosure is big, certainly compared to the Humboldts – which waddle around a little under 70cm high. When they shuffle into the water, performing that magical penguin transition from funny-little-man-bird-tottering-on-rocks to graceful-submarine-bird-flying-through-the-sea, they arc and dive together as a flock. When they return, though, it is to their own nest, and their own partner. "They constantly hang around with each other," says Schoene. "They sit in one little cave together. It's a really strong bonding."

And yes, the homosexual couples have sex. And no, Schoene has not worked out if they take turns. "It was not observed by keepers if one is more often on the bottom or top," he explains before adding, like a responsible scientist, "We have not done the statistical analysis."

Ten years on, the couples are still together – and members of the public still arrive at the zoo asking to see its famous gay penguins.

Gay penguins are not new, and nor do they only appear in captivity – but for a long time we chose to ignore them. In 1913, the explorer George Levick returned from a scientific expedition to Antarctica having performed one of the first studies of penguins, which for a century at least had been considered monogamous models of avian integrity.

The Victorians were big fans of birds, flightless or otherwise. So much so that in 1853 the Reverend Frederick Morris, an opponent of Charles Darwin, gave a sermon titled "Be Thou Like The Dunnock". He saw in their lives of monogamy and sexual probity a parallel to humans

– humans as they should be, rather than as they are.*

Perhaps this was why much of Levick's work was marked "Not for Publication". Even his notes he wrote in Ancient Greek, a last line of defence lest the uneducated masses come across them. When, almost a century later, the work was published, it was at last revealed what he was protecting them from. Between necrophilia, gang rape and reciprocal homo-sexuality by "hooligan cocks", in his words, "There seems to be no crime too low for these penguins."**

It is not just birds, though. From fellatio in bats to orgies among grey whales, homosexuality occurs throughout the animal kingdom. In bighorn sheep, who roam the Rocky Mountains like a furry mass of headbutting testosterone, it is so endemic that those sheep that don't have anal sex are considered "effeminate" by zoologists, who also note that these exclusively heterosexual males even urinate in a crouched posture – like, confusingly, females.

What's more, in humans we know there is a genetic compo-nent to it – studies show, for instance, that identical twins are more likely to be both homosexual than non-identical twins.[88]

---

* He would not have been happy to learn that dunnocks are in reality absolute filth.

** Anyone who has watched ducks at breeding time would struggle to see why he was shocked. Mallards engage in "rape flights", pursuing and copulating with exhausted females. It is a measure of changing human sexual mores that while he wouldn't publish his work for fear of its reception, one of the most celebrated zoology papers of recent years concerned the occasion a mallard engaged in a rape flight with another mallard, chasing him into a window where he died. The window belonged to Kees Moeliker, a Dutch scientist, who made it down in time to see the victorious mallard mounting, and wrote the paper that made his career, "The first case of homosexual necrophilia in the mallard". It has since been made into an opera; the aria is the opening line of the methods section – "Startled, I watched."

The conclusion is inescapable. If homosexuality is unnatural, someone needs to explain that to the natural world.

This is a serious conundrum. Imagine you had never heard of evolution, and someone described it to you. One of the most basic predictions you would surely make is that a trait that made people less likely to reproduce should die out. Male homosexuality, a trait that, at least among exclusive homosexuals, means people have no interest at all in the act of reproduction, should never have existed in the first place. And yet it does. How?

⸺

One day in 2012, a Pakistani woman called Nargis knocked on the door of a Karachi mansion. Behind her, at the end of the drive, security guards and tax officials sat in a pick-up truck. But on the doorstep, there was just Nargis – and the reporter from the *Guardian* newspaper who happened to be witnessing this particularly unusual form of debt collection.

The door, he wrote, was sheepishly opened. With a nervous glance to see if any neighbours had spotted the visitor, the homeowner accepted a bill and promised to pay. He knew what would happen if he didn't. Nargis, a member of the transgender community known on the Indian subcontinent as Hijras, would be back with a group of others like her – ready to sing, dance, clap and generally make a scene.

Qazi Aftab, a local tax official, told the reporter that this was the "nuclear option", but it was rarely necessary. "Because of the neighbours they get very embarrassed. Usually just one minute of shouting is enough and then they pay up."

It would be a gross misrepresentation to say that Hijras are accepted. They suffer severe discrimination, and many have to make their living from far more demeaning activities than Nargis. They are often seen by day begging at traffic lights, by night working as prostitutes. But, equally, they are a recognised part of society and have been for centuries. In 2004 Asha Devi, also a Hijra, was elected mayor of Gorakhpur under the slogan "You've tried the men and tried the women. Now try something different".

The Hijras are frequently referred to as transgender but the word, at least in the western understanding of it, is not quite right. In one survey of the Pakistani community, 87 per cent said they felt neither male nor female.[89] Many people argue they don't necessarily feel gender dysphoria – the term for feeling that their true gender identity is different from the one dictated by their bodies. Devi's campaign material gives a clue that they may be something else, something found surprisingly often in societies around the world – from the Khatoey ladyboys of Thailand to the Native American "Two-Spirit" people. That something else is a "third gender".

What follows is controversial. It is a theory about homosexuality, third genders and transgenderism that will manage to offend some people from all of those categories. It is easy to see why it might offend. When you have fought for so long for your distinct identity, you don't want to find it blurred into others. But even for those who vehemently disagree with the specific research focus, the lines of inquiry reveal a lot about evolutionary explanations for homosexuality. And in a later chapter, we will see how others deny this fundamental premise when applied to same-sex attraction, but use the same methods to explain another evolutionary mystery – transgenderism.

Paul Vasey, from the University of Lethbridge in Canada, believes that homosexuality as it manifests itself in most of the modern world is unusual. He thinks you can see homosexuality as it was practised by our ancestors in our evolutionary past in more ancient cultures. And in looking at these cultures that display what are today called third genders – in particular the Fa'afafine of Samoa – he believes we can find clues as to why the evolutionary paradox of homosexuality persists.

What is interesting for Professor Vasey is that, firstly, there is no recognised gay identity in Samoa and that, secondly, the Fa'afafine occur in the same proportion as male homosexuals in the west. He believes there is a simple explanation for this. "I'm gay," says Professor Vasey. "But if I'd grown up in Samoa I wouldn't look like this. I'd probably look like a really ugly Fa'afafine." He's being too hard on himself. At least from what I can make out on our Skype interview, I'm sure he'd be a perfectly attractive Fa'afafine.

Fa'afafine translates literally as "in the manner of a woman". Boys who appear more feminised in their behaviour will often be classified as a Fa'afafine, and brought up as something between a woman and a man. There is also an analogue for masculinised girls – Fa'afatama.

The fact they go on to sleep with men is not the only similarity between Fa'afafine and western gay men. "There are all kinds of traits the two share in common. Both exhibit elevated childhood gender-atypical behaviour, both exhibit elevated childhood cross-sex wishes, both exhibit elevated childhood separation anxiety, both prefer female-typical occupations in adulthood."

For Professor Vasey, it seems obvious that being Fa'afafine

and being gay is the "same trait, expressed differently depending on the culture". More than that, if you look at existing cultures closer to those in which we evolved – where humans make a living by hunting, existing in small, egalitarian groups – the third gender is the form that homosexuality takes. It is likely, Professor Vasey argues, that the oddity is the west – that the way homosexuality manifests in Europe and North America may even be an expression of our repression rather than our freedom.

"The part of the brain that controls sexual partner preference, it's the same for all of us," he says. "It's just that if you take that biological potential, put it in Samoa where society doesn't flip out about male femininity, then feminine little boys grow up to be Fa'afafine. If you take that potential, put it in Canada, feminine boys learn pretty quickly they had better masculinise to survive." This, he believes, is precisely what he ended up doing.

Whether the "third gender" really is the ancestral form of homosexuality, with the way it is practised in the west today an aberration, is a separate issue. That homosexuality can take such widely different forms shows the impact society can have on sexuality. That its prevalence remains largely the same also shows the limits of such socialisation – that there is something else going on. But what?

Professor Vasey is one of the very few scientists in the world looking at this question, and he does so thanks to the Fa'afafine. There are two specific theories used to explain homosexuality that he is interested in. The first could be termed the "benevolent uncle hypothesis".

Alatina Ioelu does not remember not being a Fa'afafine. Yet he does remember not wanting to be one. "You don't really come out," he said. "You're just that. In a way it's good, in a way it's not good. When you're growing up as a kid you're innocent of your actions, how you move or sound. You're not aware you are doing something that doesn't conform to the norms of how society considers boys." But he clearly didn't, because his classmates began to call him a Fa'afafine. "And so you grow up being known as that. I wanted to distance myself from it, I didn't want to be that." He couldn't, though, because he realised it was true. "In the end you're like, 'shit, that's what I am.'"

It would be wrong to claim that the Fa'afafine are completely accepted in Samoa. "It's fair to say that no father will jump for joy when realise at age three or four that their son is a Fa'afafine. They'll still have to come to terms with that," says Alatina.

There is a place for them, however, and always has been. "It's a normal part of society, they're everywhere. They walk around and nobody says, 'Oh, that's a Fa'afafine'. In my family we have a long line going back. I have a great uncle that's a Fa'afafine, I have four second cousins, a first cousin…"

When he heard about Paul Vasey's research, he realised that this itself was a paradox – all these Fa'afafine going back generations. "How the hell do we have Fa'afafine, and they don't reproduce? How is it we are still around, when we don't have children?"

He also realised that Professor Vasey may have the answer. Fa'afafine do not have biological children of their own. Conventionally, from the point Alatina realised who he was, he was taking himself out of the reproductive game. Or was he? Perhaps not entirely. The benevolent uncle explanation is based on the idea that there is more than one way to pass on your genes. The best way to reproduce, in terms of percentage of genes passed on, is to clone yourself through asexual reproduction. Stick insects can do this. Humans, alas, can't.

The most efficient method we have to perpetuate our genes is sexual reproduction – passing on half our DNA each time, with the other half coming from our partner. It is not the only option, though. Your siblings, for instance, share half your genes, which means your nieces and nephews share a quarter. To an uncle each of those nieces and nephews is therefore, from a genetic point of view, worth half a child. What if simply having an extra man around, a benevolent uncle to provide for the extended family's children, was enough to ensure more of those children survive to reproduce themselves?

This could be where the Fa'afafine come in. Alatina says that there are clear and defined roles for them. "They become almost like the caretakers of families. They are responsible for taking care of the elderly, parents, grandparents, even their siblings' children. Because they are feminine they take up this motherly role in families."

It is not that they are trying to become women. Unlike in the western transgender community, they are fairly relaxed about pronouns. "If you're in a group of Fa'afafine the 'he' and 'she' are thrown back and forth interchangeably. Often you don't notice. Generally Fa'afafine don't really pay attention to that stuff."

Crucially for Professor Vasey's theory, unlike women they will never have a child of their own. Having an extra hard-working adult without dependants is no minor advantage. Everyone has extra fish, extra firewood – and fuller bellies. It is not implausible that, particularly in difficult times, a childless Fa'afafine could ensure more nieces and nephews reach reproductive age.

That is the idea behind the benevolent uncles hypothesis, that good uncling becomes a form of reproduction in itself. To test the theory, Professor Vasey looks to see if the Fa'afafine are more avuncular – literally, uncle-like. He has found that, compared to single straight men or aunts, they are indeed more likely to want to look after their nieces and nephews. They take more interest in them, babysit more than straight men, buy more toys, tutor more and contribute more money to their education.[90]

Of course, in order for a gay uncle to be useful you need to ensure he, or she in the case of some Fa'afafine, actually has nieces and nephews (and preferably a lot of them) to be useful for. There's no point in being a good uncle with no one to look after. So it would be good for this theory if gay uncles were more likely to pop up in big families. Incredibly, they do. One of the best-established and more intriguing results in homosexuality research is that the more elder brothers a man has, the greater his chances of being gay.[91] The mechanism seems to involve each pregnancy leading the mother to develop antibodies against a protein involved in male foetal brain development – attacking it and so preventing it from doing its work.[92] Or, put another way, as families get more likely to benefit from the services of a gay uncle, the chances of one appearing increases.

In order for this to completely explain homosexuality, a lot of extra nieces and nephews would have to be born and survive – probably too many for the genetic mathematics to add up. If a niece is worth half a daughter, then you need two extra nieces to have survived because of you to make up for the fact that you yourself didn't have a daughter.

The theory would also have to explain why the Fa'afafine should be homosexual rather than asexual – if a gay uncle has lots of time on his hands to help out, imagine how much more one not interested in sex at all would have. But Professor Vasey does not think the benevolent uncle theory needs to be a complete explanation. It can be one of many, and the other leading contender is the "sexually antagonistic gene hypothesis", more snappily known as the "sexy sisters hypothesis".

What if the genes for homosexuality persist because despite making non-reproductive (if avuncular) men, when they appear in women they produce excellent breeders? Again the Fa'afafine, and Samoa, have been his laboratory. Professor Vasey took 86 Fa'afafine, and 86 heterosexual Samoan men. He then looked at their grandmothers – who are easier to study than sisters, because all their breeding is already finished.

He found that the grandmothers of the Fa'afafine were indeed better breeders.[93]

The theory is simple. By passing on their genes these grandmothers might end up with the occasional grandson who wears dresses and doesn't reproduce (though always remembers his nieces' and nephews' birthdays). But they themselves, thanks to the very same genes, were also better at reproducing – so made enough other grandchildren to make up for it.

There is a problem, though, given the way the theory was originally framed. Somehow, the "sexy grandmothers hypothesis" just doesn't have the same ring to it.

When George arrived at the public toilet, he was obviously apprehensive. "Situated at the window of the restroom, I saw him leave his old station wagon and, looking up and down the street, walk to the facility at a very fast pace," wrote Laud Humphreys, later. "Once inside, he paced nervously from door to window until satisfied that I would serve as an adequate lookout."

Humphreys had a role in that toilet throughout the summer months, which were known in the local community as the "hunting season". He was a "watchqueen".[94] Back in the 1960s homosexuality was still illegal in the US. He was there not to get involved but to watch out for the authorities. Later, he explained the specifics of his duties.

"A 'watchqueen,' as he is labelled in the homosexual argot, coughs when a police car stops nearby or when a stranger approaches. He nods affirmatively when he recognises a man entering as being a 'regular.'" In return for this service, he gets to watch what goes on. For Humphreys, a sociologist in a time before university ethics committees looked down on this sort of covert research, it was the perfect role.

He noticed in those toilets that one of the most initially disconcerting aspects is the quiet. Mouths, he said, seldom open – adding the qualification, "for speech".

But those toilets, quiet or not, did a brisk trade. "I have seen some waiting turn for this type of service," he wrote. "Leaving one such scene on a warm September Saturday, I remarked to a man who left close behind me, 'Kind of crowded in there, isn't it?' 'Hell, yes,' he answered, 'It's getting so you have to take a number and wait in line in these places!'"

Humphreys was nothing if not empirical. For instance, he explained, "Analysing the average age of 53 participants of fellatio, I arrived at these conclusions: the insertee was judged to be older than the inserter in 40 cases; they were approximately the same age in three; and the inserter was the older in ten instances." Many did not consider themselves to actually be gay until, reluctantly and after much soul searching, their advancing age – and declining attractiveness – forced them to make the switch from inserter to insertee.

For George, Humphreys thought this crunch moment was coming. "Weighing 200 pounds or more, George has a protruding gut and tattoos on both forearms. Although muscular and in his mid-thirties, he would not be described as a handsome person."

Humphreys allowed himself to wonder what would happen when, in the brutal market of the public lavatory, George's youth ceased to have the value that ensured he could be "inserter". "For him, no doubt, the aging crisis is also an identity crisis. Only with reluctance – and perhaps never – will he turn to the insertee role. The threat of such a role to his masculine self-image is too great."

Humphreys' research has gone down as an absolute classic in the history of sociology. Partly this is because of the lengths he went to, but also because it showed just how hard it is to study people who don't want to be studied. He provided a very rare glimpse into a hidden world. It was a world so constrained by society, though, that it is difficult to tell what those 53 acts actually tell us about human homosexuality that is relevant in the west today, or in Samoa ever.

This is the problem with homosexuality research, and to a lesser extent sexuality research in general. People want to know what our "natural" state is – how we would be without the tangled web of history and culture and society. As if, somehow, what is natural is also itself an explanation – and validation.

Yet how do you get to the root of our natures, if the cultural edifice our behaviour rests on is so intricate and varying? If people, at one point and time, can disappear for assignations in public lavatories with other men and still consider themselves straight provided they are only on one end of the arrangement, then how can you hope to tease out universal truths?

That was why Professor Vasey looked at the Samoans. His idea is that they represent, as close as is possible, our innate sexuality – before the complex constraints of modern society got in the way. Qazi Rahman, from King's College, London, is less convinced. Even if the Samoans do represent "natural" homosexuality, he is not sure the evidence from the Fa'afafine is strong enough yet for avuncularity or fertile female relatives to explain the trait's evolution, but he admits it is growing.

Nevertheless, he does think that the Fa'afafine serve one very important purpose in sexuality research. There is a fashionable argument that homosexuality is a modern creation, that it is a cultural construction invented, in part, by the Victorians in the late 1800s. Some academics argue that the idea that we each have a definite sexuality, as opposed to all of us being to some degree bisexual, is imposed by society.

Dr Rahman, who is himself gay, has no time for that idea. The fact that Samoa is a totally different society with a completely different way of understanding homosexuality, but that even there it still occurs in a defined and distinct group, shows, he says, that homosexuality can be considered a universal phenomenon. It also shows that it is possible to study it as a phenomenon while accepting that cultural influences can have a major effect.

And when I say, "he has no time for it", his specific analysis is, "I have no time for all this lefty postmodernist clap-trap." His conversations tend to go that way.

His favoured explanation for the persistence of homosexuals such as himself involves no avuncular uncles and not too much in the way of sexy sisters, although both may still play a part. He believes that homosexuality survives for the same reason other apparently deleterious traits (from a purely evolutionary and reproductive point of view) survive.

"It is perfectly possible for evolution to maintain a non-reproductive trait in small quantities if the benefits to the carriers outweigh the disadvantages," he says. Every biology student will have learnt the canonical example of this: sickle cell anaemia.

This genetic trait is, for most people, somewhere between annoying and debilitating. Those with one copy of the sickle cell gene, carriers, have blood cells that are not quite so good at taking up and transporting oxygen. Those with two copies have severely misshapen blood cells and suffer all sorts of complications. Yet the gene persists, mainly among people originally from equatorial regions. Why? As pretty much every biology textbook explains, having one copy confers a resistance to malaria – so people with one copy are, in malarial areas, more likely to reach adulthood, reproduce and pass on the genes. The benefits, in the right environment, outweigh the negatives.

Dr Rahman likes this example, because it shows the futility of talking about nature versus nurture. "It is an example of how environment and evolution are not competing explanations.

Evolution is not fixed and hard-wired." Nature interacts with nurture and vice versa.

However, the sickle cell anaemia example does not, superficially at least, seem to apply to homosexuality. After all, it's not as if homosexuals normally don't reproduce but, in certain situations – in malarial areas, say – suddenly have a massive spurt of fecundity.

But perhaps that is thinking about it the wrong way. Don't think about the person. In terms of evolution the person is irrelevant, a mere bag of ambulatory skin built by his or her genes to carry them through to reproduction. Think instead about the gene itself. It is our individual genes that want to reproduce, not us. Most of the time the goals of the human are in line with the goals of the gene, but not always.

This is the argument made about schizophrenia. Like homosexuality, schizophrenia seems to reduce people's rate of reproduction. Like homosexuality, it is at least partly genetic. How can this be? The clue may be found in a trope in popular culture – of the crazy genius, the man or woman who sees further than those who came before, but does so at the expense of his or her sanity.

The examples are many (even if not all have been formally diagnosed). Van Gogh had his ear issues, Pythagoras believed in the evil nature of beans, Beethoven had a tendency to pelt his housekeeper with eggs. Byron, considering his fellow poets, said, "We of the craft are all crazy." Millennia earlier, Aristotle had a similar thought. "No excellent soul is exempt from a mixture of madness," he was quoted as saying.

Then, even more tellingly, there are the relatives of geniuses. Albert Einstein's son, Bertrand Russell's son and James Joyce's daughter all had schizophrenia.

What if the genes responsible for schizophrenia also make you more creative? If you have them all, like Van Gogh or Einstein's son you will suffer from mental illness and be less reproductively successful. If you have only some, like Einstein perhaps, then thanks to your impressive creativity you will be more sexually successful (whether or not that rumour about Marilyn Monroe was correct…) and be spared most of the madness, but still risk passing it to your children.

A study in 2015 seemed to find just this. Looking at almost 90,000 Icelanders, it showed[95] that people who were artists, dancers or writers were also more likely to have genetic factors that raise the risk for schizophrenia. In this way, the theory goes, the genes for schizophrenia persist in the population. Most of the time, thanks to their interesting brains, the humans carrying them are better at reproducing. Occasionally, when the genes find themselves in the wrong environment – namely, a human containing too many such genes – their host does not reproduce at all.

Dr Rahman thinks something similar could explain homosexuality. Assume there are ten genes for attraction to men. "These can be expressed in women, which is a good idea." This is, in fact, a variant of the sexy sisters idea – it is possible women with these genes reproduce more. Dr Rahman says their benefits may not stop there. He extends this concept to men as well.

Like the sickle cell gene, where one copy is helpful but two is not, it could be that some gay genes can be a reproductively useful thing. It might be that if men have more than eight they are gay, but if they have fewer than eight, as with schizophrenia their character is changed in other ways which might make them more likely to reproduce.

"There's some hand waving about what gay genes may do in a man," says Dr Rahman. "One scholar said they might make men more caddish. I think that's unlikely. The homosexuality gene is fundamentally a feminising gene." So maybe instead, he suggests, although he freely admits it's speculation, having some homosexuality genes but not the full complement makes men more committed, more in tune with their partners.

These men are then better able to exploit this ability to find a niche in the mating game, passing their genes onto the next generation who, just occasionally, get the full set – and become so feminised that they stop taking an interest in women at all. No matter. So long as the extra children from the first set of men (and, perhaps, their sexy sisters) make up for the lost children from the second, the genes persist. They are, says Dr Rahman, "washed together in the tide of evolution".

Maybe what is unnatural – if the word "unnatural" means anything at all in this context – is not homosexuality, but homophobia.

A few years after Schoene discovered he had a surfeit of gay penguins, one of the heterosexual couples produced two eggs. Normally, the smaller egg would die, but the zoo instead gave it to a "really nice" homosexual couple who were still fruitlessly but hopefully nesting. They became surrogates.

And, he says, "They were a father and father but they acted like a mother and father. All the sitting on the egg and all the work after the chick hatched was shared 50:50."

The chick survived and thrived, and has now been moved to another zoo. But it spent some time in Bremerhaven first, and Schoene could watch its development. "People always ask, was there discrimination? Did it turn out differently? No, there was none. The others just treat him as a normal penguin."

The contrast with what Humphreys found could not be starker. His research did not stop at the door to the lavatory. He wanted to see these men in their "real" lives, among the neighbours and families who never suspected their hobby.

A year later, he knocked on George's door – having previously followed his car to his family house – and interviewed him under a pretext. In that setting, he found him to be a confident man. "In his own backyard, talking with an observer whom he failed to recognise, he was warm, open, and apparently at ease."

Humphreys could not help but note, as well, that leading a double life was not something that came naturally to George – that the man he had seen in the toilets was far more cautious, far more fearful, than the man he interviewed in his backyard. "After playing the inserter role with a man who had waited in the stall farthest from the door, he left quickly, without wiping or washing his hands, and drove away toward the nearest exit from the park…he was a frightened man, engaging in furtive sex."

For women homosexuality has rarely been as constrained, if only because it has often gone unacknowledged. Even so, the revolution in acceptance of male homosexuality has in some ways precipitated an even greater revolution in women – one that reaches beyond mere acceptance.

7

DIANA

Lesbians, bisexuals and fluidity

As far as I was concerned men were something you had around the place, not particularly interesting, but quite harmless. I had never shown the slightest feeling for them, and apart from my never wearing a skirt, saw nothing else in common between us.

Jeanette Winterson, *Oranges Are Not the Only Fruit*

"Vast open plains, immense spaces, eery silence" says David Attenborough, the camera sweeping magisterially across the African savannah. "The plains of our planet support the greatest gatherings of wildlife on Earth," he continues on the television in front of me.

I shuffle, bare-bottomed, in the seat and wonder how I ended up here.

The "here" in question is a windowless box in Essex University containing a large flatscreen television and a "penile gauge". The television is controlled by Gerulf Rieger, an academic. The penile gauge is controlled by me.

In 2004 Dr Rieger published a paper with a Canadian

researcher, Meredith Chivers, called "A sex difference in the specificity of sexual arousal".[96] Its consequences are still being debated today.

The study asked men and women to place their sexuality on a scale, from completely heterosexual to completely homosexual. Then, the researchers showed them erotic videos – featuring either men or women. To calm people's ardour before the videos, they showed wildlife documentaries.

There was, however, a twist. As well as asking them their sexuality beforehand, during the videos they wired them up to what some have interpreted as the sexual equivalent of a lie-detector test. Each person wore a device that measured blood flow to the genitals.

The results, for men, were dull. If a man told you he was heterosexual, then his genitals told you the same thing. His blood flow flatlined when he saw naked men, it rallied for naked women. If he said he was homosexual, the reverse happened.

For women, it was completely different. So much so that you could not even reliably tell their sexuality from their genital blood flow. When they saw either naked men or naked women the results were the same – whatever their stated sexuality, their bodies responded by preparing for sex.

A simple explanation has been offered for this apparent paradox: that most women are, to at least some degree, bisexual.

It is an explanation that, when initially suggested by Dr Chivers, resulted in her work being hailed as a rallying call for the long-suppressed sexuality of the sisterhood. Dr Rieger notes that when he made a similar inference, it was instead viewed as both offensive and slightly creepy, coming from the mouth of a man.* – like the heavy-breathing imaginings of a dodgy uncle.

This reception still rankles (not least because Dr Rieger is himself homosexual). "When Meredith came out first with this study of women's bisexual responses, she became a hero of female sexuality," says Dr Rieger. "I say exactly the same thing, and I'm somehow a sexist."

Men, on the other hand, had a less ambiguous response to the findings. "It's quite interesting, whenever I present this research to straight males I can see this glister in their eyes." They like the idea of all women being bisexual. They like it a lot.

These days, while the implications of the results remain controversial, no one doubts the findings themselves are true. They have been repeated too many times.

Now, scientists are probing the nuances of what they mean. Dr Rieger's latest research at Essex involves using the same apparatus to look at lesbian women in particular. They seem to behave a little more like men, in that they respond more to the gender they claim to be attracted to. His team is also studying genetically identical twins whose sexuality is different, to try to tease out reasons behind this.

Throughout, though, he has never come across anything to contradict the initial surprising experiments. "This is a true biological difference here between men and women," he says. "There is absolutely no question about that. The measure is

---

* Thanks to a pioneering study published in 2016, this is now a scientifically quantifiable statement. Psychologists from Knox University in Illinois interviewed over 1,000 people to produce a "creepiness scale". They found that men are creepier than women, clowns are creepier than funeral directors, and birdwatchers have a similar creepiness to porn addicts.

valid, as a test of physiological sexual responses, and it corresponds as well with what women tell us."

While women would typically tell him they were straight, they rarely did so with the vehemence of men. When asked to place themselves on a seven-point scale, with 1 being "completely gay" and 7 being "completely straight", they would typically go for a 6. Men would have little hesitation in going straight for 7.

"Woman are never as much in a box as straight men are," he says. Then, as if as an afterthought, "Do you want to see the apparatus?"

Dr Rieger's testing booth is a ceilingless box room, built inside a windowless laboratory. On one wall is a television, on the opposite a comfortable leather chair, some hand sanitiser – and a laminated notice (a lot of things here are laminated) telling you how to attach a vaginal probe or penile gauge.

Suddenly Dr Rieger has another, apparently spontaneous, thought. Later, he would admit he planned it all along. "Seeing as we are here, do you want a go?"

And that is how I end up here, shuffling on the leather seat, desperately trying not to get aroused at the sight of a coquettish gazelle. Attenborough has come as a blessed relief, after I have just – somewhat ironically – watched a man on the screen rather vigorously shuffle on a different leather seat (and do quite a lot else besides). Just as I had thought the shuffling (his, not mine) was reaching a little too frenzied a pitch, the video cut out, and a gazelle appeared.

It turns out that David Attenborough acts as something of a porn palate cleanser. "We find he really brings people down," shouts Dr Rieger, from beyond the partition. "We got really excited once; we found someone who seemed to be turned on by dolphins." He adds, a little disappointedly, "It was probably just chance, though."

⌣ ⌣

Rosie Ablewhite and Sarah Nunn are taking me through their childhood photos. There is them as toddlers: Sarah in a dress, playing with a Barbie; Rosie in a Batman suit, playing with Aladdin. There is them a little older: Sarah dressed as Wilma from the Flintstones, Rosie dressed as Fred. There is, for Rosie, a preponderance of dungarees throughout. They might be genetically identical twins, but telling them apart in these pictures is rarely difficult.

Chatting on Rosie's sofa – at the age of 29 they still live ten minutes from each other – both concede that the signs had been there, if they had bothered looking. "I've always been a tomboy," says Rosie. "I've always worn dresses," interrupts Sarah. "You have dogs, I have cats. We're kind of opposites."

"Any boyfriend I brought home instantly felt more at home with Rosie," Sarah continues. "She liked football, talked about boy things, played video games. They'd be like, 'Sarah, you're really boring. I'm going to go and play with Rosie.' I'd get jealous that they liked her better." She had a trump card, though. "When they tried to get romantic with Rosie she'd say, 'That's not me.' Then they came back."

Once, Rosie did have a boyfriend, but she found she didn't want to kiss him. So Sarah gamely stepped in. "I said to him, 'I'm the same but I will kiss you'."

Even then, the sisters didn't realise that Rosie was gay. When, finally, they pieced together the evidence, it felt impossibly strange. "I was shocked when she told me she was gay," says Sarah. "I was like, am I gay too?"

"That's why I questioned it for so long," says Rosie. "No offence, Sarah was really boy crazy."

Rosie and Sarah are some of the participants in Dr Rieger's latest research, conducted with his colleague Tuesday Watts. Drs Rieger and Watts found that childhood photographs of twins with different sexuality often show early divergence in dress. It is, Dr Rieger says, "mindblowing" that genetically identical women, raised in the same household, can "differ in something as important as sexuality".

As with male homosexuals, genetics must be involved in female homosexuality. So too must environment. If it seems strange that people still differ despite having the same genes and the same upbringing, then that is because we are forgetting that "environment" encompasses everything they encounter, including the womb. "Even identical twins can develop with different placentas," says Dr Rieger. "This means they are literally fed different substances, including different hormones. It could be that even if you grew up as identical twins, the prenatal hormonal environment still differed."

Quite what that difference is, or how it works, is unclear – and it is still equally possible something happened after birth. Lesbians are, for sexuality researchers, among the rarest groups. "Although we often think of sexual orientation as gay versus straight, amongst women bisexuality is far more common," says Dr Rieger.

He thinks lesbians are a special case. It is particularly interesting that they are the only group of women who respond in his experiments in a similar way to men – their genital sexuality agreeing with their stated one. "Lesbians are more like males. They have this masculinised genital response, with a stronger response to their preferred sex." But, he says, as with other aspects of female sexuality, much remains unknown "I still don't know what it is about lesbians, they are just fascinating."

Lisa Diamond, from the University of Utah, would agree. She has spent her career studying same-sex attraction in women, after noticing a gap in the scientific literature. "I started out in graduate school in the early 1990s and at that point models of sexual orientation were predominantly pretty categorical, pretty rigid and most public research was on men. The few articles I found based on women were more anecdotal, weren't as rigorous, and suggested a lot more complexity."

Was that apparent complexity real, though, or was it just because there had been less research? Professor Diamond began a project in which she followed a group of 79 women for ten years, all of whom had expressed some level of attraction to the same sex. She found that categorising them was a lot harder than she had expected.[97]

"Often women would have these abrupt transitions in their relationships and identity." Between interviews, they would change their own views on their sexuality – in both directions. "They weren't saying things like 'Oh I was repressed before, now I know my true self'. They were saying, 'Something happened that I didn't expect, I met this person, things got really complicated, and I don't know how to interpret it.'"

Straight women would suddenly find themselves attracted to another woman, lesbian women would find the reverse. "I had a number of women when I first interviewed them, who said, 'I was attracted to men all my life, I met this woman and the attraction was so powerful. But really she's the only woman I'm attracted to.' At first I was like, 'Is she really? Or are you bisexual?' I'd follow her over the rest of her life though, and it really was a one-off."

This effect, which she calls fluidity, was something she found again and again – there seemed to be a disconnect between sexuality as they defined it, and their behaviour. "For some women, the discovery of a capacity for same-sex attraction – or, in lesbian women, for opposite-sex attraction – came after forming a really intense emotional bond.

"They said, 'You know it's almost like the erotic feelings spill over from the really intense emotional connection.' Instead of meeting someone and being sexually attracted then falling in love, they fall in love then become sexually attracted."

"As one said to me, 'If a powerful relationship is your truth for that moment, that's your truth.'" It was like they were falling in love not with the gender, but with the person. This meant that when that particular relationship ended, and they reverted to their sexuality, they could be disappointed. "One woman was like, 'I'm kind of bummed. I hate straight culture. But I can't deny the majority of my sexual attractions are to men.'"

Is this fluidity something specific to, or at least more often associated with, women? Professor Diamond thinks it might indeed be a more female trait, but she can't be completely certain – and she thinks that Dr Rieger's genital arousal experiments only take us so far.

"They tell us something new and interesting about

sexuality and arousal, but it's not a sexual orientation tester," she says. "The basis on which most individuals make decisions about their lives and identities does not involve genital blood flow. They don't think, 'Oh I just met a great person and had coffee with them. Let me put my hand in my pants and check my genitals.'*

"So it is hard to know why we see this fluidity more in women. For instance we socialise women to say their sexuality is only acceptable within the context of an emotional bond. Men are allowed to be horny and be sexual, while we tell women that that's a slutty thing – but if you love somebody that's OK." This, she thinks, could affect the way women's sexuality manifests itself.

The statistics give us clues, though, that this might be a true sex difference. Men in the west these days have, by historical standards, extremely liberal sexual attitudes. Most are perfectly at ease with the idea of other men having homosexual encounters – but the emphasis is very much on "other men". A liberalising of attitudes has not led to a liberalising of behaviour.

Whether a retiree or an adolescent, the number of men in the UK reporting ever having had a same-sex partner hovers around 7-10 per cent.[98] As you would expect it goes up a bit with age – after all, older men have had more time to have had a homosexual experience. The only exception is that in the very oldest category the proportion drops a bit. These are the men who grew up while homosexuality was illegal.

---

* Dr Rieger, for his part, disagrees. "I consider this another sex difference. I bet most guys use their genitals to make exactly such a decision. Obviously they don't need to check, because they know– their brains and penises are so strongly connected."

But there is no evidence of a recent surge in bi-curious men among the younger generation.

The difference with women is astonishing. Their graph, initially, makes no sense at all. For the same reasons as with men, you would expect the number of women reporting ever having had a same-sex partner to increase with age. The reverse is the case. Among the oldest category just 2 per cent of women claim to have been involved with another woman. Among the youngest, it is 20 per cent.

Mathematically, the graph tells a story: that in the past 20 years women have, en masse, discovered homosexuality. The same liberalism that freed up men from homophobia about other men seems to have freed up women as well – but they have gone far beyond mere tolerance.

What is going on? Why would women apparently have a vast latent capacity for same-sex behaviour?

From a biological perspective, for women sex does not have to happen that often. In fact, humans in general have far more sex than we need. Women are only fertile for a few days a month. When they are pregnant or post-menopausal they are not fertile at all. Yet humans have sex all the time. Given most heterosexual sex is, reproduction-wise, pointless, why shouldn't a bit of the excess also be homosexual?

This is Professor Diamond's view – that exclusive hetero-sexuality may be the anomaly. "Only in the last 60 years have we had this population of same-sex attracted people who took themselves out of the childbearing market. If you look at the history of the whole freaking planet you never find that same-sex behaviour completely supplants, eliminates and replaces opposite-sex behaviour."

Sometimes, homosexuality was itself institutionalised as

normal behaviour for perfectly straight men – consider the tradition of male–male relations in the form of pederasty in ancient Greece. "As long as cultures do a good job of drawing us into conventional heterosexual reproduction, there is no real downside to being fluid," says Professor Diamond. "It doesn't have to prevent reproduction." So you can be happily bisexual, or even homosexual, and, so long as you have a smattering of successful heterosexual couplings, evolution does not care.

More than this, sex is freed up for other roles. "In social primates, sex begins to serve functions other than reproduction. It regulates emotions, and cements social bonds. Bonobos, our closest relatives, have sex to celebrate things and to make up after a fight. They have all kinds of sex. Same-sex sex, opposite-sex sex, group sex. That's what you find in complex, big-brained apes, and we are the apex of that model."

So what if, for women, same-sex activity is just a different way of socialising? This is one theory, (very) tentatively mooted by Professor Diamond. "Among our ancestors, breeding pairs didn't go to a hut and share child rearing alone like we do. Child care was shared among women. One mother would say, 'I'll go gather, you watch the kids.' Or 'I'll watch the kids, you go hunting.' This was shared activity between very close females." What if they ensured and maintained that closeness through sex? "Maybe this activity is something that unfolded in very close female bonds?"

Rosie has a less theoretical view of her sexuality. Sometimes, she says, she thinks about her mother's placenta – and whatever tiny difference it was that had such momentous consequences for her life. She also thinks about how that life would be if it had gone the other way.

"We live in a straight world," she says, speaking to Sarah. "I do look at you and think how come you get the husband? What have I done that's so different? Did I just get more testosterone? Despite being very happy with the women I've been with, any way that you look at it, it makes sense to be heterosexual."

"There are days I think you got the short straw," replies Sarah. "But there are also days I think I did. That shocks you, doesn't it? But I see the fun you and your girlfriends have together. You have so much in common." She says she still sometimes wonders about her own sexuality, about whether her identical twin could really be so different in something so important. "If my husband has pissed me off I'll say to him, 'I think I'm gay'."

～•～

"It seems to all fit OK, I think?" inquires Dr Rieger solicitously, midway through the videos. "Yes," I reply. "Good," he says. "We have extra large but I don't think you need it." And with that casual slur, another wildlife video segues into another hardcore porn video.

It's not as hard as you think to find people who make penile gauges. There's a company in the US that supplies the judicial system, where they are used to test paedophiles. Vaginal probes are harder to source, and they cost a lot more. There isn't much demand for testing female paedophiles.

The probes, as the name suggests, are also more intrusive. While the penile gauge is basically a sophisticated rubber-band-based strain sensor, the vaginal probe uses a light to measure internal blood flow directly. This is one reason why women are paid more to take part. Another is, that's what the market dictates.

"When we tell guys they can watch porn, that works. That's enough to keep them happy," says Dr Rieger. "The offer of watching erotica on its own doesn't do much to entice women. What works better for them is emphasising that this is a study into sexuality and understanding the differences between men and women."

He says paying them well is also important, simply because on scientific grounds you don't solely want to attract people who would do this for free. If your sample is meant to represent the population at large, then it is far better to know that they are motivated by money – which is a pretty universal inducement – than by putting elastic bands around their genitals. Which isn't.*

I watch another leather sofa, containing a writhing woman this time, and then Dr Rieger brings me back to some reassuring Attenborough. Is there something more complex going on with the responses? Does genital blood flow really show sexuality?

When explaining his experiments, he takes an Occam's razor view. If they appear to show most women are bisexual, it's probably the case that most women are bisexual. He says he suspects that if, somehow, we could create a new planet, where we reset all societal expectations, we would find that women wouldn't really have the concept of "straight" or

---

* There are many situations in science where it is reassuring that people are paid. In Britain, for instance, there is one solitary man employed in the role of "rectal teaching assistant". A peripatetic bottom for hire, he roams the land offering up his rear to the nation's medical students, so they can learn how to perform prostate exams. That's not the sort of situation where you want to deal with a keen hobbyist.

"gay". They would be pansexual, attracted simply to people.

That is not the only explanation, though. Another could be that most men are also bisexual, but society in the west has just been better at suppressing it, to such an extent that it does not even appear in their unconscious responses. Consider, again, the Fa'afafine of Samoa. They might appear in the same proportion as homosexuals in the west, they might exhibit similar signs of feminising behaviour in childhood, but there is something that significantly undermines the parallel between them and western homosexuals: they don't have sex with each other. Fa'afafine only have sex with "straight" Samoan men. Professor Vasey, in fact, says, "It's easier to find guys who sleep with women and Fa'afafine than to find guys who just sleep with women." While they consider sleeping with a man in a dress to be completely normal heterosexual behaviour, in the west it would, to say the least, be viewed as a teensy bit bisexual.

Dr Rieger says he would love to perform the same experiments on the Samoans to test this – but it is probably too conservative a culture for that to be possible. His view is that even if he could he would still find a clear gender difference. "I do not think that men are naturally bisexual, and that it has been socialised out of western men. Rather, I think that some heterosexual men (depending on culture) are less negative about having sex with other men than most heterosexual men are. This could be in part a matter of opportunity (if women are very conservative and not readily available for sex, or not around at all) or the fact that your sex partner looks very female, as a Fa'afafine can do, even if biologically male.

"There is also the option that some of these men who have sex with Fa'afafine are into a specific kink, as into she-males.

Our society has such straight men too; it is just not as discussed (but the porn industry knows of it)."

Professor Vasey has a similar view. In his estimation what changes with culture may not be male sexuality, but male aversion to having sex with men. In many countries self-declared straight men have sex with men – not because they prefer them, but because, like Mount Everest, they are there. "This occurs in Latin cultures, in many parts of Asia and in the Middle East where it is not seen as a big deal," he says. "It is almost as if there is less aversion to the idea of having sex with your least preferred gender in these cultural settings when you can't get what you prefer."

In such a varied and vibrant universe of human sexuality, it is not as easy to choose a neutral video as you might suspect, and not just because of dolphinphilia. In fact, there is a very specific risk associated with wildlife videos, and it is one that shows that the results of Drs Rieger and Chivers' study must at the very least be more than just proof of female bisexuality.

What if, instead of giving women a choice on a seven-point scale between completely straight and completely gay, they were given a different one where 7 was "completely and exclusively fancy humans" and 1 was "really quite into any members of the primate family"? It seems unlikely many women would say they fancied bonobos. Yet, the blood flow analysis says otherwise.[99]

If you show women videos of bonobos having sex, then you see a response. It is weaker than if it is a man or woman on the screen but it is, nevertheless, there. You might be able to make the case that all women are bisexual, but can you really also argue they are bonobosexual?

And if they are not then what else is going on? Because, Dr

Rieger explains, "It is not the case that these women want to have sex with bonobos."

He believes that this finding ties into another, which is even more disturbing. If you place a woman in a laboratory and play her the sound of another woman being chased up a flight of stairs by a rabid dog, she does not respond sexually. If you change the rabid dog for a rapist, also chasing a woman upstairs, she does. As with the bonobo video, very few women will say that they find the idea of witnessing a rape erotic. They will say precisely the opposite.

Dr Rieger takes them at their word. He thinks it is possible you are seeing an evolved response to sexual violence, developed over aeons. Put simply, in any sexual situation, whether a wanted or an unwanted one, it makes sense for women to prepare the body for sex – because, as Dr Rieger puts it, "lubrication helps minimise genital trauma". So strong is this response that it can even appear when viewing non-human primates.

When considered through that evolutionary prism, it's suddenly not that surprising that women might prefer each other. What of me, though? By the time I have seen my fifth wildlife video, and the sixth porn video, I feel there should be more than enough data to place me on the sexuality scale.

Dr Rieger invites me to peel my bottom from the leather, dispose of the gauge and come round to his computer screen. The results are in and, he says, the signal is unmistakeable. I am verifiably, unequivocally, not attracted to David Attenborough. Or dolphins.

8

HEDONE

The female orgasm and the paradox of pleasure

In regard to price, she has one fixed rule; she always measures a gentleman's may-pole by a standard of nine inches, and expects a guinea for every inch it is short of full measure.
Description for prospective clients of Miss Corbet, an 18th-century prostitute, from *Harris's List of Covent-Garden Ladies*

The assembled crowd is arraigned in a horseshoe, like student doctors observing a gynaecology examination. Just as at a gynaecology examination, Rachael Hemsi, lying naked from the waist down, is here to demonstrate an important aspect of women's health.

Unlike student doctors at a gynaecology exam, there is talk among the audience of "waves", "energy", "auras" and even energy spreading in waves from auras. We have been asked to shout how we feel. Does observing give us a "tingle" or "vibrations"? Someone calls out to Rachael, telling her he feels "a warm liquid in my belly". Rachael herself makes a sound a little like a moo.

I, perhaps alone in the room, feel neither tingly waves nor

warm auras. What I do feel as Rachael reaches climax, is extreme, profound, transcendental awkwardness.

For all the new-age talk, Rachael and her colleagues are part of a project that is helping genuine researchers. Those researchers are investigating one of the most mysterious of our physiological responses: the female orgasm.

Beforehand, Rachael had explained what was going to happen. This was to be a "symphony". Ably assisted by the hand of her fellow demonstrator Kapil Gupta, it was made clear that two professionals were going to show what it is to be at the very top of their game. So we were not to feel inadequate: this was like watching a demonstration chess match between grandmasters.

We certainly shouldn't be worried that we could not reach the same standards. Instead, we should simply marvel at the power of the female orgasm to bring people together. "Words are a really slow way of making a connection," Rachael had said. "This is so much faster."

Maybe I should be more moved, and feel less awkward. Even for scientists, the female orgasm has an air of mystique. This mystique derives from a simple conundrum. No one is sure what the purpose of the female orgasm is – or even if it has a purpose at all.

And so that is why I am here, in a first-floor North London room with the blinds firmly down – experiencing a class on "orgasmic meditation", or "om".

Om, in this room, is a verb. I om, he oms, she oms and sometimes – on special occasions – they all om together. "Would you like to om?" we role-play asking each other. "I've been om-ing for two years," says one of the teachers.

Orgasmic meditation is a practice that began – where else?

– in California, but is now firmly established on this side of the Atlantic too. Across the world, people arrange om-ing sessions, meeting in each other's houses to learn about "a spirituality practice that touches right into your very purpose", explains Rachael.

That is the real point, she says. It's not about sex (although not many people, I suspect, are asking their mothers to om), it's about connections. "The two of you together can access something you can't get on your own, and weren't taught," she says. "Orgasm speeds up your life. You can plug your life into something deeper."

Surprisingly, there is a school of science that would at least partially agree. It is now argued that the female orgasm really may have a far more complex purpose than merely facilitating reproduction.

Even before contraception, human sex was never just about reproduction. If it was then, as Lisa Diamond pointed out in the last chapter, we would have a lot less of it.

It is not just that most of the time when humans have sex it will not result in conception. It's also that they don't want it to. One study[100] that asked people their reasons for having sex found that far and away the most common purpose given was pleasure. In the same study people were significantly more likely to cite "revenge" as a motivation than making babies.

There are a range of interpretations about how this might relate to the female orgasm. At one end there is a view that in humanity's distant past we lived as free-loving matriarchies. According to this idea, which has recurred in various forms for over a century, humans existed in a sexy, fig-leaf-free version of the Garden of Eden, spending our days eating forbidden fruit and making love.

One of the corollaries of this idea, which is admittedly pretty sternly rejected by most academics in the field, is that no woman is meant to be satisfied by a single man. Instead, the female orgasm is intended to be hard to achieve in order to encourage Stone Age sexual marathons – keeping women insatiable. Some have developed an intricate explanation of all manner of human behaviour on the back of this. One extension of the idea is that the reason women vocalise (to use the primatologist terminology) during sex is in order to call more men to the party.

At the other end of the spectrum of interpretations is the rather more vanilla idea that the female orgasm is about keeping couples together – that the attention, mutual effort and mutual enjoyment ensure that men and women bond with each other to help raise children.

Diana Fleischman is a sex researcher at the University of Portsmouth, and this is the explanation she prefers – although she dislikes the term "bond". "I'm less romantic. I say what couples want is not to bond, but to control one another. Bonding is about power, and leverage."

The casual observer might wonder: why the complication? Why create these theories at all? No one is producing intricate psychosocial theories about the complex processes behind the male orgasm, after all.

The problem with the female orgasm is that it doesn't happen where it should, or when it should.

Since penetrative sex is the crucial act in producing a child, you would expect evolution to make that the most enjoyable part for women. The majority of women do not climax that way. Estimates, and ways of estimating, vary across cultures and across time. A 1933 survey of 174 women recorded that

27 per cent found sexual intercourse "highly satisfactory", 37 per cent had a "poor reaction" and 12 per cent "hate the whole thing". In a 1994 study in which both men and women were quizzed about how often the woman orgasmed, 29 per cent of women said they always had an orgasm with their partner (through any means) – a notable contrast with the estimate by the men, 40 per cent of whom thought their partners always orgasmed.

Most surveys converge on a figure of around a quarter of women always experiencing orgasm through penetration alone. Theories abound on the mechanism behind this. It may be because they have a "G Spot",* some sort of semi-mythical region inside them that produces orgasms, or it may be because their clitoris is indirectly stimulated. Even among those who do have penetrative orgasms, most still preferentially experience it through the clitoris. Most surveys also agree that between 5 and 10 per cent never have an orgasm at all.

Those who do, do so variably. So variably that one experiment, which involved observing women's brains while they orgasmed, found that those wearing socks in the MRI scanner were consistently more likely to climax.[101] The scientists' hypothesis was that they were getting distracted by cold toes.

Gordon Gallup, who researched the idea of the penis as a pump, thinks he has found a pattern in the variability of orgasm – that women are more likely to orgasm with "higher-value"

---

* One of the leading proponents of the idea of the G Spot is Beverley Whipple. So important was her involvement that at one point it was mooted this should be called the Whipple tickle. Thankfully, for this author at least, the name did not gain traction.

men. Furthermore, he has new research suggesting that, when they do, they are more likely to fall asleep afterwards – meaning that the semen has less trouble finding an egg, and they are more likely to conceive.[102, *]

As far as Dr Fleischman is concerned, it makes sense for several reasons that orgasm in women may be more variable. A man, she says, should always enjoy sex – because having sex, assuming there is a chance of reproduction, is always a good thing for him. For a woman, it isn't always evolutionarily "adaptive" to reproduce – to spend nine months vulnerable, potentially alone, then risk death during childbirth. "Evolution endows us with pleasure for behaviours that are adaptive," she says. "There's a reason for sexual behaviour to feel good. But for women sexual behaviour is not always adaptive."

So it's not surprising that female orgasms are both trickier to understand and more elusive. Crucially, it is also not surprising that they do not happen all the time, even in established relationships. Dr Fleischman thinks that their role in bonding means that if you actually attained the goal of achieving orgasms every time it would partly negate their very point. In fact, because of a quirk of human psychology, a couple would have more sex and be more likely to stay together if female orgasm continued to occur only sporadically.

"The best way to condition someone to a behaviour is through something called random schedule reinforcement,"

---

* His study involved asking college students about orgasm and sleeping in a survey. Laboratory experiments on sleeping following masturbation have also been performed, with inconclusive results, however. One reason for the discrepancy may be that the latter test used anal probes to measure the orgasms – an intervention that could wake up the best of us.

she explains. Counterintuitively, rather than giving a dog, say, a treat every time it sits, there is a school of thought that it will learn the behaviour better if the reward occurs randomly – if sometimes there is a treat and sometimes there isn't.

The same applies in gambling. "A slot machine is really reinforcing behaviour that is really resistant to extinction, because it has variable reinforcement – you never know when it will hit jackpot." So it is the very randomness that keeps people putting their resources in – to both relationships and casinos? Is that really a fair analogy? "People ask what my pillow talk is like. Well, it is a lot like that."

∼·‿·∽

Om-ing differs from masturbation, we are assured in the studio in North London, in so many ways. You don't have to do it with your regular partner. Kapil has a wife, and it isn't Rachael. Then there's the fact it is unidirectional. The om-ee is always the woman, the om-er is always the man. But the man, and the man's experience, is integral. "When you are stroking you are feeling the woman in your whole body, and opening yourself to understanding a whole new world," says Kapil.

This is why Rachael believes it is about more than sex – about "plugging your life into something deeper", as she termed it. It is, she says, "a different way of relating". For Kapil, too, there is a spiritual element. Not to mention his salary – organising the om community is his job now.

Later, I will chat to other converts to the practice, most of whom have paid several hundred pounds for the initial course, and then a fair bit more for the follow-up instructor courses. This is masturbation, monetised – using an Avon-lady model.

The devotees say it is more than worth it. They talk of being lost, of being adrift in a meaningless life. "Everything seemed pointless," says one. "I had everything I could want but something was missing," says another. Then – the punch-line of every conversion story – they found om-ing and everything changed.

Another recent convert, slightly less on-message, explains his Damascus moment to me in different terms. "I was learning meditation," he says. "Then I learnt you could do it by touching clits. And I was like, 'I am fucking in!'" He did have one concern, though. "I thought they would all be weirdos. Unlike, obviously, me."

Is there something in om-ing for the man, beyond the obvious? Could this practice have hit on the elusive truth scientists have been seeking – that the female orgasm is there to bring partners together and help them bond?

If it is, Nicole Prause hopes to spot it. Dr Prause is one of the world's leading experts on the female orgasm – a description that sounds impressive, and is, but is mitigated by the fact that there are very few people in the field. It is not easy, she laments, to get funding to investigate orgasms. Governments are wary of supporting such research in case they get bad publicity. Pharmaceutical companies aren't interested because you can't sell an orgasm.

The consequence of this is, she says, "it's a case of we don't know what we don't know". In a recent study, she realised just how much she didn't know about what she didn't know in a quite spectacular fashion. The study involved women using vibrators in a laboratory to see if they could reach orgasm.

As a back-up to the women's reports, she attached sensors to measure the contractions that came with orgasm.

These contractions have been posited as yet another explanation for the female orgasm. Could they be used to retain semen and improve the chance of conception? This is not a new hypothesis. Maria Theresa, the Habsburg empress, was reportedly advised as much by her physician, in order to conceive. "I am of the opinion that the vulva of Your Most Sacred Majesty should be titillated for some length of time before intercourse."

Even today, in Denmark pig breeders routinely titillate the less-sacred vulvas of their herd prior to artificial insemination. Whether porcine or human it's a nice idea. If orgasms help conception then consensual, pleasurable sex is more likely to succeed – in effect meaning that men who take the time to understand their partner are preferentially rewarded with offspring.

However, the evidence this actually aids pregnancy, in pigs or empresses, is equivocal at best. And that's even when contractions occur. Dr Prause found, shockingly to her, that half the sample who said they were orgasming in her laboratory had none of the physical signs. As far as her data was concerned, they hadn't orgasmed at all.

"What on earth does this mean? There is a possibility that there may be different types of orgasm and we've just yet to document them," she said. "That's the feminist perspective – to say you value the women's report over their body. It's, 'If they say they are having an experience, then by God they are – so go back and find out and make it so.' I don't share that perspective."

Instead, she thinks there's a good chance that a lot of

women who think they are having an orgasm are not. Which is a problem – not least because much of the other research so far has involved self-reports. "It's a major issue that we don't know what we are talking about."

·—·

What Dr Prause really needed, to study the female orgasm properly, was to take it out of the laboratory. "People rightly say to us that a vibrator in a laboratory is not a good model for sex. At some level you need to look at partner behaviour, bonded partner behaviours, to understand it." She needed to find a way to study orgasms in a more natural setting, but one that still somehow followed a strict experimental set-up. That sounded impossible – until she came across the om-ers.

"When first I heard of these folks doing this practice I thought, 'That's bizarre.' When they walked me through their protocol, I thought, 'My God, that's a great physiology protocol.' I'm less interested in their belief about what they're doing. I'm most interested in the genital touch. It's great for a scientist."

Om-ing is not a free-for-all. It is a ritual. There is a set way for the man to sit and for the woman to lie. His hand motion is strictly prescribed, he wears gloves, even the small talk that kicks things off is formalised (sample acceptable conversational gambit: "Your labia is light brown"). Irrespective of results the whole process must take 15 minutes – not more, not less.

The reason it is like this, they say, is to reduce anxiety in the women. If women know it will be the same each time, and have a definite end, they are better able to relax. From Dr

Prause's point of view, though, it means something else: they have controlled all the variables.

She has begun researching both parties in the om, using EEG machines to measure the electrical activity in their brains. It may be that, as well as the expected changes in women's brains, she will find sympathetic activity in the men's brains. If she does, will that mean that she has provided more evidence for the female orgasm-as-bonding hypothesis? Not in her view.

"All these evolutionary explanations, they're Just So Stories. I'm interested in data. I know people like these questions, but with orgasm I'm not sure we will ever find the answers."

For evolutionary scientists, there is an accusation to be feared in every debate. It is "adaptationist". When humans have a trait – narrow European noses, ear lobe hair on old men, female orgasm – there is a temptation to explain why that trait exists. Are European noses narrow to warm up cold air? Do old men have hairy ears to catch pathogens? Is the female orgasm a way of bonding couples?

All of those answers may be true. But there is another. Perhaps all those traits have no purpose at all. Could Europeans have narrower noses than Africans simply because Europeans have narrower noses than Africans? Maybe over millennia of genetic separation, humans' noses have gone different ways for no reason other than that's what the genes did. If big noses have no disadvantage compared to small ones, and vice versa, then noses are free to grow whichever way they so choose. Under those circumstances, constructing elaborate stories about the climatic advantage of varying nostril size is faintly ridiculous.*

As for noses, so with orgasms. Or, more pertinently in this case, as with nipples so with orgasms. Men have nipples not because men need nipples, but because women have nipples. In the first weeks of a fertilised egg, there is no sex differentiation. Later, testicles or a womb will develop, but in the early stage both sexes get the same features. And since this is when nipples appear, men get them too. They serve no purpose, men don't lactate, but the economy of biology means men have them nevertheless.

There is another part of the body shared between males and females that develops before sex differentiation: a small bud of sensitive tissue, supplied by an extraordinary density of nerves, that appears between the legs. In males, this goes on to be the penis – which is definitely needed. In females, it is the clitoris – which arguably isn't. Could it be that the clitoris only exists because of the penis? Could it be the female version of the male nipple?

Now this idea has not been popular, to say the least. It is not very feminist to argue that female sexual pleasure is contingent on an accident of evolution, less so to say that that accident is merely a vestigial happenstance of male pleasure.

But is it any more feminist to argue male and female responses must be the same? Elizabeth Lloyd, a professor of history and philosophy of science at Indiana University, is one of the most prominent proponents of the theory that the female orgasm serves no useful purpose at all. She says that

---

* This is, to be clear, an analogy. I don't wish to impugn evolutionary-nose scientists – whether or not their theories are correct is not the business of this book.

for years men just blithely assumed the female orgasm was the mirror of the male one: there, as in men, to encourage women to have sex and reproduce – without ever testing that assumption.

The result was that not having an orgasm, or even not having one with intercourse, was pathologised – something that women should seek to fix. Presuming the female orgasm had a purpose was itself sexist.

"Evolutionary accounts help define what it is to be human," she writes, in her book *The Case of the Female Orgasm: Bias in the Science of Evolution*. "Is female orgasm naturally evolved to help us maintain our pair bonds? Then that is its natural function, on the common view, and if a woman's orgasm does not accord well with that natural function then there must be something wrong with the woman – she is being unnatural."

When she looked at the data, inability to orgasm did not seem unnatural at all. Women who do not orgasm still enjoy sex, they don't have less of it – and there is absolutely no evidence that they produce any fewer children, which is surely the ultimate test. If orgasm does not affect their reproductive behaviour in a measurable way, can it really be an adaptation? If a significant proportion of women remain (to use a medical term) "anorgasmic", then is it really such a useful trait? Orgasm in women may just be a happy accident.

Or it may not. We may never establish the empirical truth about the female orgasm.

Back in the orgasm lesson Rachael Hemsi believes, however,

that with the female climax there is a different sort of, non-empirical, truth. "Desire," she says, "is the feminine face of God. It's a connection we all need in our lives. It's a God-given need to have this connection, which we need to be alive. You just feel better afterwards."

Scientists might sniff, but there is undoubtedly one thing they could learn from the orgasmic meditatees. Dr Prause believes that there could be all kinds of ancillary benefits to orgasm, in terms of mental health and even improved sleep. Research into these possible benefits is hampered, though, because there is no money in it. "There is nothing to sell."

Unless, of course, you are Kapil and Rachael. Between their intensive courses, residential courses and coaching courses they have undoubtedly achieved something science has not. They have made orgasms lucrative.

9

HERA

The power, and wrath, of the older woman

I told my mother-in-law that my house was her house, and she said, "Get the hell off my property."

Joan Rivers

Did Edward II stop to wonder, as his bottom felt the faint glow of the approaching poker, about the purpose of older women in society? As the first royal bottom hair singed and crumpled in the heat did he ponder upon the evolutionary mystery of the menopause?

If we are honest, probably not. Certainly by the time, according to contemporary accounts, his executioner inserted a "hoote brooche…thro his secret place posterialle", he would not have had the spare brain power to consider the shifting reproductive allegiances of post-fertile women.

Which is a shame because Laura Betzig, an anthropologist and historian, considers him a prime example of a hidden force too often ignored in the rise and fall of empires, in the collapse of kingdoms and in the occasional death by hot poker. That force? Older women.

If the female orgasm is a riddle, the female menopause is a riddle wrapped in an enigma. Older women should not exist, at least in the form they do among humans. Most people never think about how odd the menopause is. It is experienced by some whales, and possibly a few other primates – at least when they live longer in captivity. And that's about it.

It makes sense that it would be rare. From the point of view of evolution, organisms have one purpose: to reproduce. Yet among humans, half the population spends a third of its life or more unable to do just that.

Why? One answer is that it is just sheer chance, an evolutionary happenstance. Humans, in this view, evolved to live longer because men who did so reproduced more. But while their sperm kept going, women's eggs could not keep up. A woman's reproductive abilities stop at around the same age as those of a chimpanzee: the difference is a 50-year-old chimpanzee then dies.

Another answer is that the menopause is the mirror image of another unusual human trait: long childhoods. If a mother dies (for instance in a late childbirth) then any young children she already has may die too. If, however, she has a period of being non-reproductive that matches the time taken for her last child to reach adulthood, then that child's future is assured. If a mother has her last baby at 40, she will be likely to live until it reaches 20. If she has her last one at 60, she won't. According to this theory, then, the purpose of the menopause is to ensure that a woman's final child has a mother around until it doesn't need one.

Dr Betzig agrees with this. "In any society, children without mummies die," she says. "So they have to live a little while after their last birth." However, she thinks that something else is going on as well.

The most popular current theory to explain the evolution of the female menopause relates to looking after the interests of a woman's offspring not only in childhood, but into adulthood too. It is called the "grandmother hypothesis".

The idea is that just like gay uncles, post-menopausal women keep reproducing vicariously – in this case by making more grandchildren.

Imagine if older women evolved to be wholesome grannies – cooking, cleaning, offering their childcare experience. We in the west can all see the benefits of such behaviour – it is very nice to have an extra trusted relative to bake cakes, cluck around grandchildren and offer up opinions on colic. However, the impact through history could be far greater. In a famine, for instance, an extra forager could be the difference between life and death. In those circumstances, evolution could begin to favour grannies.

To test this idea, researchers have gone to the people they go to whenever they want to test such ideas: the Ache of Paraguay and the Hadza of Tanzania. These two tribes are considered among the closest living examples of our hunter-gatherer past still in existence. What this means in practice is that they live a life cut off from modern civilisation and the 21st century, except for the near-permanent encampments of anthropologists and evolutionary biologists who spend their lives bothering them and studying them.

The data from both groups shows that grannies are useful to mothers – helping them with food but, more importantly, also helping more of their children survive to adulthood.[103] It is not just in hunter-gatherer societies that this can be seen.

Elsewhere, scientists have looked at parish records of births, deaths and marriages in 18th- and 19th-century Christian communities, and found the same.[104]

It is a lovely idea that fits in with our idea of the archetypal granny, fussing around in the kitchen and suggesting the occasional dubious home remedy for mumps.

What if this theory could be extended, though? Evolution does not care how you achieve a goal. You could make your own line more fecund by taking on nanny duties on a Friday and buying extra baby clothes, just for instance.

Or, if you are Queen Isabella of France, you might take a rather different approach. A more poker-based approach. That is the theory of Dr Betzig, who has noticed an unusual pattern among monarchs – of which Queen Isabella is just the clearest example.

By the time the poker made its way into his bottom,* Edward had been estranged from his wife, Queen Isabella. But the marriage reached a stage that would today be termed "irretrievable differences" when Isabella, operating from France, issued a proclamation calling for the people of England to rise up, then landed with a small force in the east of England and marched against her husband.

Queen Isabella had personal reasons to hate her husband. When she married him she was just a girl, and she must have lived with the whispers at court about his true sexual leanings – his liasons with the notorious rake Piers Gaveston, then later with a new favourite, Hugh Despenser.

One contemporary noted the king "felt such love" for Gaveston that "he entered into a covenant of constancy, and

---

* Allegedly. The means of death is disputed, although a majority of historians accept he was murdered.

bound himself with him before all other mortals with a bond of indissoluble love, firmly drawn up and fastened with a knot". Another merely stated he was given "too much to the vice of sodomy".

But Isabella had another good reason to want him dead: their son. It is this reason that, Dr Betzig says, is too often overlooked. After Isabella's successful invasion, the mysterious death of her husband and the not-so-mysterious death of Despenser – who was hanged, drawn and quartered* – their son could reign as king unopposed. In the same year that the posterial poker did in his father, Edward III – and more importantly the 50 per cent of his genes that were Queen Isabella's – was crowned.

This would have been hugely to her advantage, and is a dynamic often missed in evolutionary analyses, argues Dr Betzig.

Courtly life doesn't appear to favour wives. For most of history, women in a royal palace have been part of a harem – whether formal or informal. The official wife cannot have vast numbers of offspring, and gains no genetic advantage at all from her husband making babies with other women. If he has a baby with another woman, he is spreading his DNA – but not hers. But while court cannot benefit wives at that stage of the baby-making process, it can later on – when they are already mothers and grandmothers. Provided, that is, it is their son or grandson who is exploiting the pleasures such a life affords.

"A court is full of attractive young women," says Dr Betzig. These young women give the king sons and heirs. The

---

* According to Froissart's account, it was even worse. Despenser was punished "according to his faults". "His shameful parts were cut off, his heart ripped out and thrown onto the fire."

problem is, when those sons grow up, they become competitors. "Kings are delighted to have a son, initially. But they are not at all delighted when the son comes of age and says, 'Get lost.'" The queen, however, has an entirely different set of motivations.

"The mother says, 'I am not interested in controlling a harem.'" Once she has had all her children, her pride might be hurt by an infidelity, but it is biologically irrelevant.* Her priorities have changed and instead, Dr Betzig explains, for a queen, "What matters to me is not that my husband, who is not related to me, continues to whore around. It's that my son does.'"

So her priority is to make sure it is her own son who is the only heir.

Dr Betzig has studied Britain's monarchs. At least eight queens of England had husbands die in suspicious circumstances. Or more than suspicious. Some may have used poison. Others raised armies against their husbands, or hired assassins.**

Dr Betzig found, admittedly with a somewhat rarefied sample, that you were statistically more likely to meet a sticky end as monarch if your wife was powerful – if, for instance, she was a queen in her own right. In these British cases, four of the eight were heiresses, six daughters of kings. She has

---

* Perhaps for just this reason, studies have found that women are more concerned about emotional fidelity versus sexual fidelity, compared to men.

** Not just in England. In 18th-century Morocco Zidana, a legendary wife of Moulay Ismael proved why she was his worthy favourite. When another wife vied for his affections – a young ingenue of "extraordinary beauty" – she had her strangled to death to keep her own son first in line.

gone further, and concluded that this one principle – the mother's motivation to fight against her husband for her son – may well have consistently altered the course of history.

Because there are three clear consequences of this theory. The first is that there is a good reason why women would want to gain social status and a power base. There's nothing more frustrating than realising you want to sodomise your husband to death with a poker only to then find you can't compel someone to do it. Those who argue that competitiveness is solely a male trait, related to men's need to win mates, are missing, among other things, the need for mothers and grandmothers to machinate on their children's behalf.[*]

The second is that if you happen to be married to such a woman of machinations, you should probably be careful. Just ask Henry Stuart, who died after Mary, Queen of Scots, his wife and mother of his son, had him blown up. Allegedly.

The third consequence is that the "grandmother hypothesis" just got a lot darker.

The point is, though, whether quietly plotting or quietly baking, in all these situations post-menopausal women are not just hanging around waiting to die. Their longevity is not merely a pointless evolutionary fluke.

No one writes epic poems about the travails of older women. No one composes sonnets in their honour. Their love affairs go unnoticed, their political manoeuvring is caricatured and reduced to the stories of crones in fairy tales. But, so unobtrusive that it often goes unnoticed until centuries

---

[*]   This is not just about sons either. In 1991 Wanda Holloway, a woman from Texas, hired a hitman to kill the mother of her daughter's cheerleading rival, who she believed had herself been scheming to keep Holloway's daughter off the team.

later, their effect on society – and on their own genetic legacy – is vast. Invisibility is not the same as powerlessness.

Yet, until very recently, they were ignored – by science as well as society.

⁓_⁓

Sometimes, statistics tell a story as vivid as that of any novelist. Even, or perhaps especially, when those statistics relate to chlamydia. In the past two decades, sexual-health practitioners have gained a new age group to worry about. Choose whatever sexual disease and whatever measure you want – the uncomfortable (for some) reality of increasing elderly amorousness cannot be avoided.

In the UK, one in seven new cases of HIV are now among 50-70-year-olds. In the US, annually over two million recipients of Medicare – the health plan for retirees – used its entitlements to receive free STI checks, about the same number who went for colonoscopies.[105] They were only being prudent: in just the four years between 2007 and 2011 chlamydia cases among that demographic had gone up by a third, syphilis by a half.

There is a general consensus on the cause of this. The babyboomer generation, who used the arrival of one little pill to start the first sexual revolution, are using the arrival of another pill to start a second one.

In 1998, on the problem pages of a US newspaper, readers were invited to consider a rather thorny conundrum. "I'm a 70-something widower living in a retirement complex," the anonymous letter began. "I'm outnumbered by single women by something like eight-to-one. Through no fault of my own, my female neighbours are making repeated overtures, and now that Viagra is out there, I'm anxious to give it a spin. My question is, given the close quarters, how can I be discreet?"

Viagra has changed everything. As early as 2000, just a few years after its arrival, lawyers began discussing its ramifications – whether it would be offered on the health service, but also what it would mean for the duty of care of doctors and nurses at care homes. What if one party has dementia, for instance? No one had had to consider this before.

In the *Elder Law Journal*, Christopher Julka, an editor, wrote a paper titled "Viagra as Pandora's Box for the elderly".[106] He predicted it would fulfil a deep human need, and at the same time precipitate huge social and legal changes. "Prior to the discovery of Viagra, many men found sexual potency to be an elusive quest. For thousands of years remedies consisted of grinding rhinoceros horns, chopping bear gall bladders, and dicing ginseng. Success came with modern methods, but many seemed barbaric. These included injection of medication into the base of the penis prior to sexual intercourse, vacuum pumps, and penile implants. Faced with these options, many men chose to remain impotent."

But the consequences, he argued, would not be limited to men. Instead, as the generation who came of age to the Beatles reached the autumn of their lives, they would show that they could do retirement differently too. With hip replacements to keep them flexible, beauty treatments to bolster their self-confidence and property portfolios to make sure they made the best use of their leisure time, they would – he argued – "sustain the vigour of youth".*

---

* This is not the only purported side effect of Viagra. Recently there has been concern about a potential link to skin cancer. It turned out, though, that correlation was not causation. Viagra probably does not

Even he could have not have predicted that that vigour would result in an incident in 2014 in a notorious Florida retirement community, in which an elderly woman was arrested for having public drunken sex. This came four days after she had been arrested for being drunk in charge of a golf buggy. Rather than being chastened by this, the community celebrated by naming a cocktail in her honour: Sex on the Square.

Later, reporters boasted of going "undercover" in the community – reporting on it in the same way that they might an out-of-control student drinking society. "A die-hard crowd of 60- to 70-year-olds hang out in the twee town squares openly drinking booze in plastic cups. The unofficial leader of the late-night gang used to be a perma-tanned retired biology teacher, who called his manhood Mr Midnight," explained one article.

One man told the reporter, "The older women throw themselves at the men and sex in public happens a lot. This place is just awesome."

In the same year, in an opinion piece in the *New York Times*, Ezekiel Emanuel, a senior doctor, warned that things were getting somewhat out of hand. "Combine retirement communities, longer life, unfamiliarity with condoms and Viagra – and what do you get? You get an STD epidemic among the Social Security generation that rivals what we imagine is happening in those 'Animal House' fraternities."

The point is, while the little blue pill might have fulfilled an unmet need in men, it would have been useless if there hadn't been a corresponding unmet need among women. Just

---

cause skin cancer; it's just that the kind of man who takes Viagra is more likely to hang around beaches bronzing in his Speedos.

because they are infertile, it does not mean women are not into sex. Just because they are grannies it does not mean that they will only go about asexually provisioning grandchildren and/or committing homicide with hot pokers.

Yet, until extremely recently, that was the implicit assumption in most research. In major studies such as the UK's National Survey of Sexual Attitudes and Lifestyles, older people were initially just left out. In psychology studies, they still are.

No one has ever asked a brisk gentleman on his way to a bridge game to proposition ladies of a certain age in the street, saying, "I've noticed you around the bingo hall. I find you very attractive. Would you go to bed with me?" Nevertheless, that same experiment, always conducted among men and women in their early twenties, is sometimes presumed to be a model for human lifetime sexuality.

Particularly regarding women, that seems odd. How might their responses change after they no longer have to worry about pregnancy? Even more interestingly, how might they change just before they cease to have to worry about pregnancy? If a 20-something is still, in the game theory of evolution, on the lookout for the best man with whom to pair her genes, is the 40-something simply looking for a last hurrah – applying the same logic men use all the time to argue that at that stage any baby is better than none? We simply don't know, because the research has not been done.

There is a problem that is increasingly recognised in psychology. It is that many experiments, even the canonical ones, are "weird". So the criticism goes, the subjects of too many psychology experiments are university students. That means they are Western, Educated, from Industrialised, Rich and Democratic countries. Weird. They are, in other words, a very bad proxy for the world in general. More than that, they are also young (if "weirdy" was a word, this would have undoubtedly made its way into the acronym).

Sharron Hinchliff, from the University of Sheffield, is one of a small, but growing, group of sex researchers looking to de-weird the discipline, in spite of general scepticism about the chance of success. She asks older people about their sex lives. "I remember in 2001 I was sat in with the research ethics committee at a local hospital trying to get approval to interview older people about sex for our study. Some were sat shaking their heads, 'Will people talk to you about this?' I said, 'Yes, let us try!'" she says.

And they did – and were grateful for it. "A few times I have had older women say to me, 'Ooh, I've never told anybody that before in my life.' And they probably never will again."

Sometimes, the stories Dr Hinchliff has heard have confirmed stereotypes about older generations. More often, they have confounded them. Sometimes, they have done both. "I have heard some interesting things: older women wanting to buy vibrators but unsure of where to get them from, others saying that they had their first orgasm in their seventies, following an unsatisfactory sex life with their husbands."

Again and again, Dr Hinchliff says that she found that women were grateful to talk, and had things to talk about. "This assumption that women get older and lose interest in sex because of the menopause, I've found that really not to be true. Older women are engaging in and enjoying sexual activity today. I'm sure they were 50-100 years ago too; it just wasn't talked about."

In 2015, there was another article on this subject in the *Elder Law Journal*. It felt like a companion piece to that initial speculative warning from 15 years earlier. Nursing-home sex is, today, a serious and mainstream topic. In Britain, the Royal College of Nurses has released a discussion document, advising care practitioners on the dilemmas it throws up. What if one party is not mentally capable? What if neither is? Should family members be consulted? Or privacy respected? No one yet has the answers.

This particular paper was about when the owners of care homes become responsible for sexual, as well as geriatric, health, and was titled, "Nursing home liability in the senior sexually transmitted disease epidemic". It didn't make as grim reading as that suggests, though.

Alexander Warso, the lawyer who wrote it, began with a little vignette depicting the new reality of life, for some, in nursing homes. It seemed that, to prepare his readers for the legalese that would follow, he wanted to depict the new reality of aging – to puncture any stereotypes they might have. Although arguably he went a little too far with his tale of George and Vera.

If they had met a generation earlier, George and Vera – the couple he invented to help add colour to his story – might have met at a milk bar, and maybe cemented their relationship at a parish dance. Then, in the twilight of their years, they could have looked forward to carriage clocks, elasticated waistbands and growing old together.

Today's George and Vera, however, became socially conscious amid the protests of '68, danced to Hendrix at Woodstock in '69 and had no intention of staying with anyone for life – or of going quietly into the good night.

Instead, in Warso's imaginings, they began their relationship at a nursing home.

"As the clock struck nine, Vera shuffled down the hallway," began Warso, in an admittedly unorthodox start to a legal discussion document.* "She could feel a tingling running up her spine from excitement and anticipation. Really, the tingling was from the friction of her slippers on the thick, dark carpet, but she was in too much haste to notice. Vera stole a furtive glance back at the door to her room as it slowly creaked shut, and she froze with fear and anticipation as she waited to make sure none of the staff noticed her out of bed.

"As she neared George's door, she gently slipped down one hand over the handle while she undid the ties on her blouse with the other. She quietly slipped in, carefully closing George's door, before shyly whispering: 'George, you awake?' 'Yes,' George answered, 'come on over.' George sat awake on top of his adjustable bed in his flannel pajama shirt and trousers. 'Come here, you,' he coaxed ever so gently as Vera slipped in bed alongside him…"

Of all the liberalising trends in human sexuality that George and Vera had seen in their lives, none perhaps would have seemed more revolutionary than that which appeared to occur only at the end: the push for greater transgender awareness. For all that it would have seemed like a new movement, it was anything but.

---

*   The *Elder Law Journal* is brilliant. Seriously. It's basically beach reading.

10

ISHTAR

Misfits and inbetweeners: the hidden history of transgenderism

My vulva, the horn,
The Boat of Heaven,
Is full of eagerness like the young moon.
My untilled land lies fallow.

Ishtar

The goddess Ishtar peers out from the terracotta with an uncompromising take-it-or-leave-it air. "Have you got a problem with me standing naked on a pair of lions while flanked by two owls?" she seems to ask. "Well then, go find a less fabulous goddess. There are plenty in the Greek gallery."

Four thousand years ago, you didn't mess with Ishtar. She is the Mesopotamian goddess of…well, it's complicated. "She's sex, but she's also war," says Jon Taylor, assistant keeper of the British Museum's cuneiform collection. While the Romans had Venus to deal with matters of the heart and Mars to watch over them at war, the Mesopotamians combined the two.

This may be because different city states had different gods and over time they joined the two by accident. It could also be because they did not see them as so separate. "There's an idea it's a result of a patriarchal society embodying uncontrolled female power," says Dr Taylor. "Ishtar is dangerous, because she is not someone's wife and daughter." And obviously, for precisely the same reason she is extremely alluring.

Either way, if men are from Mars and women are from Venus, then Ishtar is from both. And her followers seemed to know it.

"The cult of this goddess included all sorts of people who were in some way unusual," says Dr Taylor. "She had ecstatics, who go into a trance, people who had knives and cut themselves, and people who had some kind of different gender identities." It is difficult, across the millennia, to work out what this means – but these followers are repeatedly referred to in a specific way in the cuneiform tablets: woman-man.

"One of her powers was to change men into women, women into men," says Dr Taylor. Her followers, according to the cuneiform writings, were females who carried weapons like men do, and males who weaved like women do. "It looks like if you were one of those people who doesn't fit into their equivalent of our binary genders, if you are anything in the middle, then she was the goddess for you."

<hr />

Sex did not begin, whatever Larkin would have you believe, in 1963. But Larkin was only wrong on the details: sex did "begin". And the point at which it began, in some rather adventurous eukaryotic cells, was between 1.3 and 2 billion years ago. Before then every organism that had ever lived, a grand line of continuous reproduction stretching back at least the same length of time again, had made a copy of itself directly without having to consider the messy business of finding a mate.

Why this changed remains contentious. Sexual intercourse seems like a very bad idea, as a reproductive strategy. The whole point of reproduction is to pass on your genes. If you reproduce asexually, you pass on 100 per cent of your genes. If you reproduce sexually you lose half your genes by mixing them with your partner's.[107, *] You also have to find a partner, and persuade that partner that he or she is pleased to have found you. Most evolutionary models would suggest that asexual reproduction, where you need neither dilute your genes nor spend time finding someone to dilute them with, is a better strategy every time. Those initial freak cells that went sexual should have been bred out of existence. Instead, their descendants went on to inherit the Earth.

The leading argument as to why they won out is that this gene shuffling creates and maintains more genetic diversity. Asexual reproduction produces identical offspring, which will be identically wiped out in a plague. Sexual reproduction shuffles them up. So while in the short term asexual organisms proliferate, sexual ones are better able to keep one step ahead of their parasites. Happily, they also then prove to be better able to adapt to changing environments – to sea level rises, ice ages or acidification.

But that is not the mystery that concerns us here. The mystery we need to resolve is not sex, but sexes. Why are there

---

* Assuming there are two sexes. But we will come on to that.

two sexes?* Sexes are not what you might think they are. They are not breasts and genitals, or even X and Y chromosomes. And way back then, at the start of sex, they probably did not exist.

I am going to tell you a story. It is one path, of many, that could get us to the world we have today – a world of males and females.

When those first organisms decided to reproduce sexually, they did not magically create male and female. In their Garden of Eden, at the beginning of sexual reproduction, there was not Adam and Eve. There was something quite a bit more ambiguous.

The process of sexual reproduction involves getting the DNA out of one organism into a place where it can meet the DNA of another organism, without it getting eaten. The mechanism humans have evolved for doing this is what we call sex – with half the humans putting their DNA into a small gamete called sperm, the other half into a big gamete called eggs. But there is no reason it has to happen inside a body.

In this early world, it didn't. Organisms met, fused their DNA and created life. In this early organism – let's call it unisexius – there was only one gamete size, and it was the same for every member of the species. A tiny bit of this was DNA, the rest was food for the growing embryo. A version of this still exists in yeast.

At some point between unisexius and *Homo sapiens*, half the gametes of the species got small and became sperm and half got big and became eggs. Why?

---

* Just as intriguingly, why are there equal numbers of both? For this, look up a beautiful bit of game theory, called "Fisher's principle".

Here is one answer. Suppose some of the members of unisexius by genetic fluke made ever-so-slightly-bigger gametes. On the one hand, this is harder work. On the other, it might be worth it if their growing foetus does better – because it has more food.

This has an unintended consequence, though. If some produce large gametes, others of this species could get away with making smaller ones. Provided they could find a way to only fertilise the big ones, there would probably still be enough nutrition for their offspring. What's more, the energy saved in making small gametes would mean these freeloading members of the species could make more of them, giving them a better chance of achieving that fertilisation. Maybe some of the energy saved could even be directed towards making those gametes mobile, giving them the ability to swim. They could have, say, a tail like a tadpole.[108]

So it is, perhaps, that the brief utopia of unisexius collapsed under its own inherent instability – pushed towards two extremes in size. Until, today, we find ourselves in the situation where a human egg is 10,000 times the size of a sperm, and big enough to be visible to the naked eye.

That difference in size, and only that, is what defines the sexes. When biologists say that an organism is male it is because it makes small gametes. When they say it is female it is because it makes big ones.

Everything else comes after. In humans, it happens that the male sex is determined by a single stumpy bit of DNA, called the Y chromosome. Our genetic data is parcelled up into 23 pairs of chromosomes, which are shuffled up during sexual reproduction, and re-paired with those of our partner. The final pair is the sex chromosomes – in girls there are two large X's, in boys there is a big female X, aligned with a runty male Y.

But even something as apparently fundamental as this is not a definition of sex. In some species it is the female that gets the different chromosome.

Viewed this way, it is not so strange, at least in theory, to believe that our brains need not follow our bodies. It is not so ridiculous, in other words, to believe that sex – the gamete size – and gender – the behaviour aligned to it – can be separated. This is the argument of the transgender community.

Here is another story. When a male canary is hatched, it emerges from its egg into a cacophony. Amid all the sounds and sights of its new world, it needs to pick out something in particular: song. The songs of male canaries are passed down the patrilineal line. The less-complex songs of the females are not. So not only must the new chick learn a tune, it must know which gender to learn it from.

Joan Roughgarden, an evolutionary biologist from the University of Hawaii, has an idea of how this might happen. Maybe they learn the male song because their brain has a filter. What if they crack open the egg, stick out their beak and are able to sieve out the competing sounds of females, to concentrate only on those of males? The song comes to them as a form of canary culture, but the mechanism to receive that culture is biologically determined.

If this is so, then it is conceivable that some canaries could be born male, but with the filter tuned to the wrong sex. They would then grow up singing like a female. They would be, to all intents and purposes, transgender canaries.

Professor Roughgarden would love to find a bird that sang with the other sex's song, not because she is especially interested in birds – but because the animal world still has a rhetorical power to affect human debates. Thus transgender canaries could validate transgender humans in the same way gay penguins validate human homosexuals.

"It would have the effect of telling people that this is something that happens in nature," she says. "It is not a myth, not something people are making up." What would be even better would be to identify the part of the canary's brain that is different. "When you have a structural correlate, you can say, 'Oh well, this is not a figment of our imagination, not some story.'"

In the past decades, as "LGB" has gained an appended "T", it has felt as if we've been in a gender revolution, a fundamental reimagining of what it is to be a man or a woman or neither. Those in the trans community would prefer to categorise it not as a reimagining, but as a rediscovery.

⌣ ‿ ⌣

Al Dalal was not, by most reasonable measures, "ladylike". In one story, it was said that he farted during prayers and excused himself with the words, "I praise thee fore and aft".[109] In another, he bedded both a bride and a groom on their wedding night – separately convincing each that they needed to cool their ardour with him first for the sake of the other.

In a very specific sense, though, he was indeed ladylike. He was a member of the Mukhannathun, a group of effeminate men in seventh-century Arabia who fulfilled a role similar to those found in today's three-gender societies. In early Islamic descriptions, they wear women's clothing and are prized for their musical abilities. More than that, though, they form a bridge between the sexes – able to associate with both men and women.

Elsewhere, there were also signs that the men-women who once followed Ishtar still kept a foothold in society. West of Arabia, Augustine of Hippo, the Christian theologian who famously said, "Lord, make me pure but not yet," complained of the temptations offered by such people, who in that society were followers of the goddess Berecynthia. "I listened to singing boys; I thoroughly enjoyed the most degrading spectacles put on in honour of gods and goddesses...On the yearly festival of Berecynthia's purification the lowest kind of actors sang in front of her litter, songs unfit for the ears of even the mother of one of those mountebanks, let alone the mother of any decent citizen."[110]

But these groups, who always lived on the edge of society, eventually found themselves pushed right over that edge. Their castes, still present further east in India, all but disappeared among the monotheistic societies.

Al Dalal himself saw the beginning of the end, when Islam tightened its grip and the punishment for his kind became castration. Even then, at least according to one supposed conversation, he and his fellow Mukhannathun seemed to be philosophical. "With castration I have become a mukhannath in truth!" said one. "Or rather we have become women in truth!" replied another. A third said simply, taking a consolation that clearly didn't apply to Al Dalal, "What would we do with an unused weapon anyway?"

Then, their kind disappeared.

In the diaspora of Ishtar's people over the centuries, those who were born as female but felt more masculine vanished even sooner. Sometime between the cuneiform of Mesopotamia and the scrolls of classical civilisation, their caste faded from the record. Theirs became a truly secret history far earlier.

Sometimes, with hope as much as scholarship, famous women from history will be claimed for the cause. Perhaps Queen Hatshepsut of Egypt, who wore a false beard and male clothing, was an early example of gender fluidity? Or Joan of Arc, who was burnt at the stake for, among other things, dressing as a man? Or the women of the 18th century who disguised themselves as boys and joined the Royal Navy? The problem is, there are very good reasons to gain power or access by pretending to be a man, even if you are perfectly happy being a woman.

Just occasionally, though, a less ambiguous case will appear, surfacing from the great depths in which it had hidden, like a coelacanth of gender. Take Harry Gorman, for instance. For 20 years Harry worked as a US railroad cook, living and passing as a man. Then, in 1903, Harry was hospitalised and the truth was discovered. Still, Harry refused to conform, declaring that "nothing" would persuade her to wear women's clothing. She* said there were "at least ten other women" she knew of who lived similar lives, and they would often socialise together.[111]

In Britain, Charley Wilson almost completely got away with her deception. Born Catherine Coombes in 1834, she lived as a man for most of her life, before being forced into a poorhouse aged 63. There, she was found out and forced to wear a dress. She remained defiant. "If I had money," she said, "I would get out of here in men's clothes and no one would detect me."

---

* In these examples I've been forced to make a pronoun choice. Both options seemed unsatisfactory. "He" feels anachronistic, not least because Harry referred to "women". I went for the birth sex.

Transgender people, then, have always been with us. But never in great numbers, whichever historical period you choose. Of the children who attend clinics that treat people with gender dysphoria, around 80 per cent will find that the feelings go away after puberty.[112] The remaining 20 per cent will join the estimated one in 300 people who identify as transgender, those in our society who sing with the other sex's song.

If only we could look inside their heads we might be able to see clues as to why. Ironically, while it is pure speculation whether there is a "structural correlate" of transgenderism in canary brains, there is increasing evidence, albeit disputed, that there is one in the brains of humans. This is despite the fact, says Professor Roughgarden, that the same is not true of homosexuals.

"You see this continual argument about the gay brain," she says. "People find it, they don't find it. Usually, that's a tip-off there's nothing going on. They just want to find it. In contrast there's not a lot of argument about the transgender brain."

One part of the brain is very different in men and women. Known as the bed nucleus of the stria terminalis (BSTc), it is typically twice as large in males as in females.[113] Two crucial studies involving postmortems of transgender people found that among men who believe their gender identity is female, it is smaller.[114] Among women who believe their gender identity is male, it is larger. In other parts of the brain there are differences too. Generally, those differences follow the same pattern: the brains of transgender males are more similar to those of females, and vice versa. But all this work comes with the caveat that the numbers of people investigated are very small – transgender people are rare, transgender people who agree to have their brains examined after death rarer still.

Finding something in the brain is not the same as interpreting what it means – or even establishing whether the structural changes in the brain cause the transgender behaviour, rather than the reverse. Our understanding of the brain has improved dramatically in the past century, but that's a bit like saying that our understanding of the dark side of the moon has improved dramatically in the same period. It is still an alien land. So this does not explain transgenderism; what it may tell us, if it was ever doubted, is that it's real.

Does that mean that gender is unimportant? If you can be either/or/in between, do these distinctions mean anything at all? Of course they do. It is strange to think that those who claim gender to be a social construct would ever use transgender people as evidence to support their belief. If gender were not important, then we would not have transgender people – people willing to go against every structure in our culture to declare themselves born the wrong sex. There are few decisions someone can take that are socially more difficult. Professor Roughgarden, who was born as Jonathan in 1946, knows that better than most.

"In my age group, the whole idea of being trans was unthinkable. Even being gay was unthinkable. So I spent many years trying to live as a male, but I just didn't...enjoy... what men do. I enjoy what women do."

It was not until middle age that she finally decided to change sex. "It's about not being able to do the things that other people find natural. Not being able to laugh when other people laugh, not being able to enjoy sports with other men, not knowing how to dress. It's not feeling comfortable in men's circles, but not having access to discussions and confidentialities with other women. Eventually, it leads to a sense of profound loneliness. I just got to the point where I thought, I've tried this for 40 years, and I can't figure out how to be a man."

One particular, utterly tragic parable has been used to show how strong gender identity can be. Which is especially ironic because it was originally used to prove precisely the reverse.

In 1973 John Money, one of the most distinguished gender researchers of his time, gave a speech that changed the discipline for ever.

Professor Money had made his name working with children born with ambiguous, incomplete or the "wrong" genitalia. The number of people estimated to be transgender is low. But there are several times as many for whom gender is still not quite as simple as X and Y.

Some of these children might be genetically female, in that they have two X chromosomes, but with a condition that means they are overexposed to male hormones* – leading to enlarged clitorises.

Others might be XY boys who don't have enough receptors for androgens such as testosterone. Still more could have Klinefelter syndrome, in which a boy is XXY, with an extra chromosome, and often goes on to have a lower sex drive and a smaller penis and testicles. It is estimated that 1-2 per cent of people have some disorder of sex development. But most

---

* These girls have been of particular interest to sex researchers because they appear to show more male-gendered traits, such as rough play – which they link to testosterone.

are mild – only a hundredth of that figure have ambiguous genitalia.[115]

Back in the 1970s, Professor Money would make the parents of such children a promise. He could mould their children into whatever gender they wanted to be. They could be assigned to the sex that seemed most appropriate, and with surgery, therapy and hormones would grow up happy and well-adjusted.

One of those sets of parents was the Reimers, from Canada, who had seen Money on television and gone to him in desperation. Bruce, their baby son, had a malformed penis, and they wanted to make him a girl. That was exactly what Money did, as he had for many others before. Bruce became Brenda.

Two things were different about this case, though. The first was that the cause of the malformation was not hormonal or genetic, but human – a botched circumcision. The second was that Brenda had an identical twin brother.

As Professor Money gave his speech that day in 1973, when Brenda was seven, the scientific audience instantly understood the significance. You could not have designed a better experiment into the malleability of gender. If two children with identical genes, from an identical womb, could be nurtured to diverge in something as important as gender, then gender itself was dead.

For the next quarter of a century, the case seemed settled. Until, one day, another sex researcher thought it would be a good idea to follow up with Brenda. Brenda no longer existed; by now she was called David.

The attempt to change the child's sex had been a catastrophe. When Brenda came home her parents had, following

Professor Money's instructions, dutifully treated her as a girl – giving her dolls and dresses, and keeping the truth a secret. Professor Money had visited to continue the therapy, forcing the twins to act out bizarre sex roleplay, in the belief that such play as children determines future roles.

But Brenda never felt like a girl. She eschewed the dolls in favour of toy guns. She fought with, and regularly overpowered, her brother – who later said, "I recognised Brenda as my sister. But she never, ever acted the part." Her classmates called her "caveman". She started oestrogen supplements, but stopped them at the age of 14 and confronted her father – she was convinced she was a boy. He broke down and confessed. "For the first time everything made sense," she said, "and I understood who and what I was."

The damage, though, had been done – and not just to Brenda. Over the years, thousands of operations have been performed on people with ambiguous genitalia, often assigning them to their non-chromosomal sex. If the abnormality is hormone-related, studies have shown that people often feel happy in their assigned gender. If the abnormality has some other cause, then the outcome is often much less positive.

Brenda decided not to take her birth name when she changed her sex back. Instead she chose David, after the story of David versus Goliath – trying to draw on some of his strength. David went on to get married, adopting three children. He never found normality though. In 2000, he told a reporter, "You can never escape the past. I had parts of my body cut away and thrown in a wastepaper basket. I've had my mind ripped away." Four years later he committed suicide.

"Why," asks Professor Roughgarden, "do we insist on genitals as a marker of gender?" In other cultures, they don't. "Go to societies like the Polynesians and Native Americans, and they don't see gender as connected to genitalia." Their transgender people often see no need for an operation. "There it's linked to occupation. If you are a woman you do women's things. If you're a man, you're a warrior."

Today, for all that we consider ourselves enlightened, people who are transgender in the west often have a stark choice. To be legally accepted as having changed their sex, in many countries they need to first pathologise themselves. They need a diagnosis of gender dysphoria. They need treatment, possibly surgery. They need to declare that they are abnormal. Professor Roughgarden calls it a "pact" that people make; denying themselves to become themselves.

However it is handled, trangenderism is clearly natural. In the trivial sense, that is a tautology – its existence is proof enough of its naturalness. So too is its long and extended history. The big question, as with so much else that does not fit in sexuality, is: why? Many people who transition from male to female and vice versa claim simply that they have the wrong brain in the wrong body. But not every answer is quite so simple, or so politically palatable. And it is a measure of how little we still undersand about transgenderism that the theory with the strongest backing among sex researchers has nothing to say about one half of the world's transgender people, and is roundly rejected by most of the other half.

Anne Lawrence is, like Professor Roughgarden, a sex researcher who also happens to be transgender. One day, she came across work that completely changed her view of herself. "I experienced a kind of epiphany...It spoke to my experience like nothing I had encountered before," she said. That work was by Ray Blanchard, from the University of Toronto – and it is fair to say that Dr Lawrence is rare among the transgender community in appreciating his contribution.

Blanchard has a theory that the people who are born man and change sex fall into two groups: homosexuals and heterosexuals. For the first, changing their sex may be simply a manifestation of their sexuality. If homosexuality itself is a feminising trait, they are an extreme example.

For the second, a significant proportion of the male-to-female transgender population, there is something more complicated going on. After all, if you are a man and attracted to women, why change your sex only to become that most niche of minorities, a transgender lesbian?

His answer is that such men are not so much attracted to women as attracted to the idea of themselves as a woman. Professor Blanchard has collected case studies of men who, before changing their sex, became aroused at the idea of menstruating. They were turned on by the idea of lactating, of having breasts and wearing women's clothing.[116]

These people are, he argues, "autogynaephilic" and their behaviour has all the characteristics of a paraphilia – a sexual abnormality.[117]

For all the controversy, Dr Lawrence found others who agreed with the theory, telling the story of one subject who, after changing sex, wanted to have sex with a boyfriend – not because she fancied him but because it validated her as a woman. "She stated that she felt no particular attraction to men's bodies, but was only interested in the way in which being with a man sexually made her feel like a desirable woman. Asked whether this meant that her male partner functioned primarily as another 'fashion accessory' with which to enhance her self-image, like a pretty dress or a designer handbag, she replied that this metaphor expressed her feelings exactly."[118]

Most members of the trans community did not have quite the epiphany Dr Lawrence experienced. The research was treated, she says, as "not so much wrong, but heretical. The intensity of the reaction was astonishing. It was as though thinking about transsexualism as a sexual problem involved such a paradigm shift that it frightened people".

More than that, the research directly challenged the concept of sex and gender as separate. Transgender men are not women trapped in men's bodies, according to Blanchard's and Lawrence's research. They are not looking at the world through a female filter. They are just another manifestation of male sexuality.

⌣‿⌣

Professor Roughgarden is one of those who opposes Blanchard's interpretation – describing some of the arguments used in its support as "hate speech". She looks to other researchers to explain transgenderism. Specifically, she looks to Paul Vasey, who studies the Fa'afafine to understand homosexuality. She thinks his research is extremely useful – and its conclusions completely wrong.

"There are researchers who are gay, and insist on seeing

the Fa'afafine as gay. For them the Fa'afafine's gender expression is incidental to and instrumental in realising their gay identity," she says. "People try to capture them." She wants to capture them too – not for homosexuality research, but for transgender research.

Professor Vasey considers the Fa'afafine's "uncle-like" behaviour to be a validation of theories explaining the nurturing benefit of gay uncles. Professor Roughgarden argues otherwise. She says that if it walks like an aunt, looks like an aunt and clucks around its nephews and nieces like an aunt, it probably shouldn't be called an uncle. They aren't gay, they're trans – and the research gives a clue as to why such people exist at all. "Uncles don't do what Fa'afafine do, aunts do!" says Professor Roughgarden. "Hello?!"

In the late 1990s, a routine excavation of a fourth-century Roman site in Yorkshire happened upon a grave filled with wonderful treasures. There was a jet necklace with matching bracelet, a shale armlet and a bronze anklet. There was also a paradox – although the skeleton was wearing women's clothing, the body was of a man.

For Pete Wilson, an archaeologist from English Heritage, it was extremely exciting. "He is the only man wearing this array of jewellery who has ever been found from a late Roman cemetery in Britain," he said at the time. He also knew why. Earlier, an altar had been uncovered to the goddess Cybele. Another name for Cybele is Berecynthia: the goddess whose followers had so delighted and shamed Augustine.

Cybele was worshipped by a class of priestesses, the gallae, all of whom started life as men. Initiations into the cult happened in the spring, when candidate priestesses scythed off their own genitals in an ecstatic frenzy, then left them on the doorstep of a house – whose female inhabitants gave them women's clothing in return.*

It is possible to trace the family trees of classical gods. We know that the Greek god Poseidon is equivalent to the Roman god Neptune. The Egyptian god Amun-Ra was considered by the Greeks to be equivalent to their god Zeus. Cybele, scholars believe, traces her roots to a more obscure goddess from a more obscure civilisation: Ishtar.

So it is that thousands of miles away in Yorkshire, and two thousand years later, we find the echoes of the Mesopotamian cult of Ishtar. And now, another two thousand years on, the echoes can be heard still.

Human sexuality, then, can be squeezed, suppressed, restrained or denied. Ultimately, though, it cannot be significantly changed. Or can it?

---

* What equivalent use they found for freshly severed genitals is less clear.

11

HYMEN

The mystery of marriage

Montesquieu, who is really a fellow of genius too in many respects; whenever he wants to support a strange opinion, he quotes you the practice of Japan or of some other distant country of which he knows nothing.

Samuel Johnson

One day in 1996, a boat containing two British police officers dropped anchor off the coast of Pitcairn. From the deck they watched as a longboat set off from the remote rocky island. This boat was their only route to dry land, and they were somewhat suspicious of its occupants.

"The men looked quite frightening – knives on their belts, hair all over the place, no shoes on," one of the officers later told reporters.[*] "They came up the rope ladder on the side of the ship. It made me think: Where are we going?" Where they were going was an island where, they would learn, sex came with different rules – or no rules at all.

---

[*] For more on this read the excellent feature "Trouble in Paradise", in *Vanity Fair*.

Over 200 years earlier, the great-great-great-great-great-great-great grandfather of one of those unkempt shoeless men had himself had a similar experience as he dropped anchor off a different island thousands of miles away. Fletcher Christian was one of the crew of the HMS *Bounty*, making him among the first westerners to see Tahiti. By the time he arrived there, though, it was already legendary in Europe.

Sailors spoke of naked women, swimming up to greet European ships. Captain Cook described a ceremony where "a young Fellow above 6 feet high performed the rights of Venus to a little girl about 10 to 12 years of age publickly". His surgeon spoke of "exceedingly beautiful" women who "used all their arts to entice our people...they absolutely would take no denial".

They found that they could buy sex in exchange for iron nails – a discovery that soon threatened the structural integrity of the ships.

In this exotic Eden, captains complained of the difficulty of keeping their men in check. In 1768 Louis Antoine de Bougainville, the explorer who brought back the Bougainvillea plant to the west, wrote, "I ask you, how was one to keep four hundred young French sailors, who hadn't seen women in six months, at their work in the midst of such spectacle?"

They were right to be concerned about controlling their men. HMS *Bounty* never reached Britain. Instead, Fletcher Christian and his shipmates mutinied – taking over the ship and sailing with their new Tahitian wives to a new settlement, on the remotest speck of land on the planet.

Two hundred years, and feminism, can change your perspective. On Pitcairn, Polynesian rules – or a corruption of them – still applied in the late 20th century. But these days they had a different designation. This wasn't a free-loving Eden, prosecution lawyers would maintain. What went on on modern Pitcairn was mass rape.

Just 47 people lived on the island and, initially, when those British detectives landed they were charmed by the residents – who played the part of the cheery, simple natives. In their pidgin, this was an accepted tactic. "We hypocrited them," they would say.

But the detectives were not completely taken in. The investigation by the British government, whose jurisdiction technically runs to Pitcairn, and which began with that visit, eventually resulted in the incarceration of a third of the adult male population of the island.

Testimony collected from women who had left the island was shocking. They described routine under-age sex. Girls were taken into the bushes by older men; pregnancies and abortions in early teens were common. At the age of 12 or younger, girls were "broken in". The sex involved the married and single alike. One woman told the court, "I don't know any married couple on Pitcairn who were faithful to each other."

Steve Christian, Fletcher's direct descendant, was implicated in five rapes. It was appalling abuse, and it was society-wide.

But when the world's press arrived to report on the trial, they found their moral certainties challenged. A gathering of women, much of the adult female population, made the argument that it was not appalling at all.

Many of the women talked of their own "breakings-in". "I thought I was hot. I felt like a big lady," said one. "I wanted it as bad as him," said another. Their point was, this was their culture. Who was Britain, a nation against whose moral code their ancestors had mutinied to escape, to judge?

If this was their informal case for the defence, Desmond Morris, the eminent anthropologist and zoologist, became their expert witness. "The crucial thing about the Pitcairn people is that they have reverted to a primeval tribal community," he said. "There's virtually nothing to do. They fish and get food and sing songs and have sex. Life is that simple, back at the level of a primitive human tribe when there was nothing wrong with a post-pubertal girl having sex because that is what biology intended."

Was he correct? Possibly. Although whether that meant Britain should not prosecute is a different question. Just because something is natural, it doesn't make it right. And just because an island seemed to be a paradise of carnal delights to sex-starved sailors 200 years ago, it does not mean that we can't question whether it felt such a paradise to the voiceless 12-year-olds with whom they were carnally delighted.

﹏

It can be depressing to be a married man writing a book about human sexuality.* What hope is there for marriage when human nature seems to be set against it? How can lifelong exclusive love persist when two thirds of men will assent to a random offer of sex in the street, and when married women will covertly seek sexier genes once a month, and when our bodies themselves seem designed for infidelity?

---

* My wife proofread all my chapters. At this section she left a note, "I tell you: that is literally nothing to what you feel being the wife of that married man reading it."

What hope indeed. Of the half a million Britons who each year make a solemn oath to have and to hold, from this day forward, for better, for worse, for richer, for poorer, in sickness and in health, until death do us part, more than 200,000 will fail.

Yet there is a converse to that statistic. Despite the temptations of Tinder, the snare of extramarital sex and the privations of parenting, almost 300,000 will succeed. Monogamy, for them, works. The odds as they stand on that altar are not so awful after all.

Why do any succeed? It is not a silly question. Why do we, in the west, call ourselves (however fuzzily we might define it) a monogamous society? Is marriage the natural state of humans? Or is it a shackle? Were our ancestors polygamous? Promiscuous? Should men have harems? Should women? To answer these questions, over the years evolutionary scientists and anthropologists have engaged in a strange parlour game. They have tried to construct the original, true human society.

For some, it is clear that our Stone Age past involved pair bonding. Matt Ridley, the science writer, cites the theory of a primatologist called Richard Wrangham, who thought that cooking led to pair bonding. "Cooking requires you to gather food and bring it to the hearth, which would have provided ample opportunities for bullies to steal the fruits of others' labour," he writes in his excellent book *Nature via Nurture*. "Or, since males were at that time much bigger and stronger than females, for males to steal food from females. Accordingly, any female strategy that prevented such theft would have been selected, and the obvious one was for a single female to form a relationship with a single male to help her guard the food they both gathered."

Others believe the precise opposite to be true. "*Homo sapiens* evolved to be shamelessly, undeniably, inescapably sexual. Lusty libertines. Rakes, rogues and roués. Tomcats and sex kittens. Horndogs. Bitches in heat," write Christopher Ryan and Cacilda Jethá, in their phenomenally successful book *Sex at Dawn*.

They look to what happens among our nearest relatives – bonobos. These peaceful primates, they contended (wrongly, many primatologists now argue), rarely stop having sex. They have sex because they are happy, because they are sad, to say hello, to say goodbye, to cement friendships and – just occasionally – to reproduce too.

For Ryan and Jethá, we were the same until the rot set in with agriculture. Only with fixed communities did property become important – and with it inheritance, patriarchal control, the violent exercising of power and all the other ills of humanity.

Some look instead to existing societies for inspiration. Perhaps, like 85 per cent of hunter-gatherer tribes, we are meant to be mildly polygamous.[119] We could even be like the scattered Himalayan communities that practise polyandry – where two brothers marry one wife, and together work, uncle and father, father and uncle, in the harsh high-altitude environment to eke out resources for their shared children.

Or should we take inspiration from the Na of China? Anthropologists love the Na because they provide a counter-example to almost any societal norm you choose to define as universal. Feminists love the Na because the way they achieve that is by a subversion of male power.

Here, in the remote Yunnan hills, children have no fathers. Women live with their brothers, and unrelated men just come for the night – arriving after dark to consummate their "walking marriage", then leaving at dawn. In this society, lineage passes from the mother, and men have no control or claim on their children. Is this relict population the last reminder of what unfettered human sexuality looks like with women in control?*

All these questions are not as unanswerable as they might seem. Humans descend from a very small group of ancestors. There is less genetic variation among the entire 7.5 billion global population than there is among chimpanzees. Precisely because they were so small in number, we cannot make reliable inferences about what that tiny band of ancestors did. They may have hunted and gathered, with men taking down deer while women picked berries. They might have lived by the sea, with both sexes working cooperatively to collect fish and crustaceans. Even so, some hypotheses about our evolved sexuality can be ruled out.

The size of testicles is a good indicator of promiscuity: the more sperm a species produces, the greater the likelihood that sperm is competing with other sperm to fertilise an egg. So the fact our testicles are bigger than those of gorillas shows that humans did not evolve in a society with total fidelity. The fact they are smaller than those of chimpanzees also shows that we did not evolve in a society with complete and unfettered promiscuity.

The overall difference in size between male and female animals of the same species is a good indicator of polygamy. Male sea lions are three times the weight of females, and the successful ones control large groups of them. Gibbons

---

* They are not, though, as some contend, a true matriarchy. Men still hold political power.

are monogamous, and males and females are the same size. So the fact that human males are about 15 per cent heavier than females implies that, polygamy-wise, we are somewhere between sea lion harems and gibbon marriages – but closer to the latter.*

Contrary to the theories of *Sex at Dawn*, it seems exceedingly unlikely that we once lived as free-loving naked apes, enjoying our nakedness together in peaceful but lusty matriarchies where everyone shared parenting and parentage. For one thing, primatologists now think much of the bonobo behaviour that we thought was natural was caused by captivity. For another, recent research has shown that even among bonobos not all sex is equal – the top males still produce the majority of the offspring and the females still get to choose.[120] Amid an apparent free-for-all, the same dynamics come through.**

There is also a piece of psychological evidence that suggests our ancestors formed marriages, rather than lived unattached lives: the fact that we find beauty in youth. Chimpanzee males do not especially favour younger females. Why would they? An older female is more experienced at raising young.[121] The fact that humans do suggests that they are in it for the long haul. Men who gain a lifetime mate at a young age also gain her fertility for a longer time.

Other research has shown that our past cannot have been a peaceful Eden either. The earliest cold case is the skull of a hominid, known romantically as "cranium 17",

---

* This does not mean there is no pressure on women to get larger too. Larger mothers may produce healthier children.

** What apparent free love there is can also have darker overtones – for instance as a way of placating aggression. Recent estimates suggest bonobos have as much sex as chimpanzees.

who, apparently, fled to the back of a Spanish cave 430,000 years ago – before having said cranium smashed in. He was far from a one-off. One of the commonest breaks found by archaeologists in the bones of our distant ancestors is a "parry fracture" – the characteristic shattering of the left arm that occurs when someone holding a weapon in his right arm shields himself from a blow with his left.

The archaeological* evidence shows that male violence and power struggles (quite possibly over women), have existed for as long as humans themselves. The anthropological evidence shows that, with notable exceptions, the majority of hunter-gatherer societies have some form of marriage – but also that that marriage is normally polygamous. The biological evidence shows that infidelity has always been with us.

The question is, if multiple marriage is so common, why in the west did monogamy – or an imperfect version of it – win out?

It is a question that Joe Henrich, from Harvard University, has spent quite some time considering. "We don't look like monogamous apes," he says. That this isn't our natural milieu is clear from even the most cursory look at how bad we are at monogamy. "You can see monogamy doesn't fit with human nature. Society struggles with divorce. High-status men have serial marriages – they might only have one wife at a time, but they have lots of them, like Larry King and Donald Trump.

---

* And, recently, genetic. An ingenious 2016 paper traced the common ancestral lineage of homicidal behaviour in different mammals – and found that homicide rates varied from 0 in bats to 12 per cent in wolves, with primates like humans at a "natural" 2 per cent rate. By showing that our homicidal impulses were shared with other related species, the paper argued that the trait of human violence predated humans themselves.

That's human nature pushing back against our legal system and social norms, and trying to pop out of it in different ways it can."

The triumph of monogamy is especially surprising, he wrote in a paper analysing this conundrum in 2012, "since the very men who most benefit from [polygamous] marriage – wealthy aristocrats – are often those most influential in setting norms and shaping laws. Yet, here we are."[122]

Why? The best answer is that, economically at least, monogamy makes societies a lot more successful.

⌣–⌣

The Asia-Pacific Society of Cardiology Congress is an annual jamboree for the region's heart doctors. Every other year, this caravan of cardiologists sets up in a different city. The scientists who attend get a professional excuse to visit some of the most beautiful locations in Asia. And then, generally, they go into a windowless and impersonal conference centre to discuss statins.

In 2017, they went to Singapore and saw the botanic gardens before reviewing research on heart stents. In 2013 they went to Thailand and saw Bangkok's floating market before considering the latest data on obesity. In between, for the 2015 congress, they were in Abu Dhabi – and that was when one of the groups of local scientists decided to present some more location-specific research.

Dr Amin Daoulah, from the King Faisal Hospital in Saudi Arabia, had noticed an unexpected trend among his male patients. There was one lifestyle factor that increased the risk of them suffering a heart attack fourfold. That factor?

Having more than one wife at the same time. What is more, the more wives they had, the worse it got.

In Deuteronomy, there is a note of caution for those looking to engage in polygamy: "He shall not acquire many wives for himself, lest his heart turn away." This research seemed to show it was even worse than that. Multiple wives do not just make your heart turn away, they make it pack up altogether.

This was especially surprising because in the west, one of the best things a man can do to improve his health and life expectancy is get married. But, Dr Daoulah argued, it seems that you can have too much of a good thing, wife-wise.[123]

"The need to provide and maintain separate households multiplies the financial burden and emotional expense," he said. "Each household must be treated fairly and equally, and it seems likely that the stress of doing that for several spouses and possibly several families of children is considerable." So considerable that, whatever the Arabian Nights fantasy, the reality can be deadly.

Brent Jeffs knows all too well the reality of keeping different wives and children happy. Born into a fundamentalist Mormon family, he was one of those children. And he is tired of dealing with the "harem fantasy" perception of what that life involved. "Outsiders tend to think our form of polygamy must be a great deal for us men. You get sexual variety without guilt: in fact, you are commanded by God to have multiple partners and the women are expected to go along with it," he wrote in *Lost Boys*, his book about his experiences.

"To many men, that sounds like heaven right there,

without any need for the afterlife part. They focus on the sex – fantasizing about a harem of young, beautiful women, all at their beck and call. They don't think about the responsibility – or the balancing act needed to keep all of those women happy, or even just to minimize their complaints."

He said that, in his family, providing for basic material needs was a challenge, let alone the actual parenting bit. "Simply keeping dozens of children physically safe is close to impossible." He estimated that one in five of his fellow families had lost a child, often due to accidents caused by lack of supervision.

The statistics suggest that figure is not far from the truth. One study found that the risk of premature death among children from polygamous marriages is 7-11 times higher than those from monogamous ones.[124] Again, this leads to an inversion of accepted truths in monogamous societies. In most of the world, children born into richer families do better. In some polygamous societies, the reverse happens. A bit share in a rich dad is worse than the full attention and investment of a poor one who can only afford a single wife.

The wives are, unsurprisingly, not happy with a bit share either. In the Bangwa tribe of Cameroon, there is a saying: a house full of wives "is like a handful of poisonous snakes". Other polygamous cultures have similar folk idioms. "A pair of dogs always bite", "pecking hens never agree".

There is a naïve idea in cod evolutionary psychology that men compete and women passively await the victor. Then, once marriage occurs, the game is over.

Tell that to the Iatmul people of Papua New Guinea. One appalled anthropologist visited and wrote of how "co-wife fighting is the most vicious fighting I have ever witnessed in the village. And it was the most frequent". It involved anything to hand: knives, shovels, spears, sticks. It would take weeks to settle down. "Eventually," the anthropologist noted, "they tend to reach a sort of hostile pragmatic indifference."

In 2005 William Jankowiak, from the University of Nevada, collected such accounts, to show the reality of inter-wife conflict. Sometimes, a marriage would result in full-on battles. "Whenever a new wife enters the family it is common [for them] to exchange insults for a time and then begin pulling, tugging, and beating at each other," recorded a visitor to the Alorese in Panama. "Immediately all the women of the village become involved. Each wife has a certain number of belligerent allies, and in addition there is always a large group of women who try to separate the combatants but who manage in their role of peacemakers to land some very effective blows. A whole village may be in a turmoil of struggling women waging a shifting warfare in the mud or dust of the dance place for as long as from two to four hours."

Sometimes it would be more targeted. In the West African Bamana people, "it is common for a senior wife to success-fully force the departure of a co-wife through use of black magic, thereby causing considerable anxiety for the remaining co-wife". In Tonga, "it is believed that co-wives often resort to various love medicines in an attempt to gain first place with the husband and that they may use sorcery to kill a hated co-wife or her children".*

---

* Of course monogamy does not guarantee a lack of marital violence. In the Middle Ages in Germany, there was a formalised duelling process for husbands and wives looking to settle their differences. To even up the contest, the wife would be given a rock and the husband would be buried to his waist in a pit with one arm tied to his chest at the elbow.

Such fights can appear semi-comical, but they shouldn't. This is, directly or indirectly, about their children's lives. Becoming the favoured wife can be crucial for their health and happiness. It can give them the power to protect their offspring, and do the reverse for their fellow wives. In general, children living with an unrelated parent are between 15 and 77 times more likely to die 'accidentally'."[125]

So it is not surprising that even when fighting is not overt, conflict is continuous. Among the Dogon of Mali, the language has even been adapted for this purpose. "Co-wives translate their sexual jealousy into fierce insults whose secret goal is to cause the husband's distaste for the other wife." Many of these insults focus on their rivals' genitals comparing them, in one especially vivid simile, to a "hyena's foot".[126]

Translate this into the western world and it may explain the findings of studies into the simmering and sometimes toxic politics of teenage female friendships, particularly when it comes to undermining love rivals. While men compete overtly, women seem often to do so surreptitiously, deviously, and are in it for the long haul – a strategy perfectly suited to a harem.[127] A 2008 study found that the more attractive a girl was the more likely she was to be victimised.[128] With boys the reverse was true. Another found a similar dynamic with clothes. The more provocatively an attractive woman dressed, the more likely she was to suffer negative reactions from other women. Women gossip more, and do so in ways that undermine their "competition".[129]

So polygamy is bad for children. It is bad for wives. It is arguably bad for husbands. But there is one group missing for whom it is catastrophic – single men. This is because of what Brent Jeffs refers to as "the math problem". "Half of all children born are boys, of course," he says. And if one of those goes on to have five wives, four of his peers have none.

Most Mormons are, these days, monogamous. For over a century the mainstream church has banned plural marriages. But a few pockets of resistance remain – one of which was Brent's church. When he reached adolescence he found himself part of that "math problem", and also one of the solutions brought to bear to deal with it. He was expelled from the community.

He was not the only one. Boys are kicked out for all sorts of infractions. Listening to CDs, playing video games, being disrespectful. Others just leave – realising their prospects in the church, where elders monopolise the young women, are poor. In the outside communities that receive them they are called the "lost boys". In 2016, one such lost boy pointed out to a reporter how it was odd that they never seem to expel girls.

The lost boys are, in the wider human history of polygamy, an oddity – they have a monogamous society to flee to. Most polygamous societies are not tiny enclaves amid a monogamous mass. This, says Professor Henrich from Harvard, is the most significant problem with polygamy: it creates disenfranchised, disenchanted young men with nothing to lose.

"Imagine lining up all the males according to status. If you are in a monogamous society, there is roughly one woman for every male," he says. "If rich guys take extra wives, though, you end up with this pool of low-status males. Being in that pool changes your psychology and how you think about the world. You take risks – because you have to climb up that status ladder."

This is not just theory. In China, the one-child policy and selective abortion meant that there was a large rise in the number of males – leading to a near-doubling of the number of unmarried "surplus" men. Crime rates doubled too. In India, where sex-selective abortions are also a problem, sex ratio strongly predicts murder rate. "The effect is large," wrote Professor Henrich. "Going from a male to female ratio of 1.12 (in Uttar Pradesh) to 0.97 (in Kerala) cuts the murder rate by half."[130]

Viewed like this, when Boko Haram and Isis, both supporters of polygamy, raid a Yazidi town or a Christian village, is it surprising that the young fighters make off with the women as "wives"? Whatever the ideological cover, they are war bands motivated by a bounty so primitive it feels they can trace a direct line back to their cavemen past.

Monogamous marriage pacifies men and women. It results in more investment in children from fathers, and fewer young men roving in bands destabilising society. Looking across the world, it is correlated with civil liberties and democratic rights.

The result, Professor Henrich believes, is that on almost every measure monogamous societies do better. To which you might say, fine – but that still does not explain why we have it. Societies where everyone pays their taxes do better too, but that does not mean they exist. And polygamous societies still make more children.

The difference, argues Professor Henrich, is that monogamy becomes self-perpetuating, a form of cultural evolution. It may be an unnatural arrangement but, once established, it flourishes – and is imitated. "It is natural for a society to look at a country or city that is particularly successful and say, 'Hey, what are they doing right?' and copy their institutions," he says. "Laws surrounding monogamy spread throughout the 19th and 20th century. They were copied by Japan in

1880, Turkey in 1926, China in 1953, Nepal in 1964."

He calls this process "self-domestication", and it is something unique to humans. "Culture creates these environments with institutions, norms and laws, and if they make people successful they flourish."

The question is, if the way human sexuality is organised can change so much once, could it change again?

12

MUSES

Culture, context and the future we choose

In order to suppress sexual passion, I entered the faculty of mathematics.

Response to Moscow student survey, 1903

It is the quiet that feels strangest. No one ever told me that orgies could be so quiet.

On the wall above us in a sex cinema, the organisers are playing a movie depicting a threesome. There, things are very different. The actors' professional orgy is far from quiet. Indeed, the synthetic grunts of their brightly lit bacchanal rise as one, in anticipation of some sort of epic synchronised climax. Everything you could want to see, and everything you could want not to see, is illuminated by studio lights – a harsh, shadowless, melee of flesh.

Below, our actual orgy has sprung up as if in sympathy. And the real thing, illuminated only by the pinkish light of those on-screen thighs, is a far less vocal and visible affair. Occasionally, someone coughs. At one point there is a whispered question from an onlooker. The whispered answer must have been in the affirmative – he moves a hand into the melee, onlooker no longer.

Siobhan had warned me I might initially find it all a bit much – that my first exposure to a proper swinging party could feel a little overwhelming. "It's a fantasy world, and that can be a bit full on," she had said. Siobhan, in her fifties, is my guide to this community. She has been "playing" (a term I initially find disconcerting, but which eventually comes to feel apt) on the scene for a decade or more.

"I really enjoy it. I enjoy the fact it's my secret life, something I do that my friends don't know about. In my teens and twenties I had a high sex drive that was difficult to manage, so I took to this like a duck to water. This is a place where you can realise your fantasies," she said.

That may be so, but at first it was the mundanity of the situation that struck me.

From the horseshoe of onlookers around the heaving heap of bodies in the cinema, someone shifts forward, to see if he can enter the privileged circle of participants. Throughout, he keeps his gaze fixed on proceedings – staring with all the intensity of Kasparov during a chess game. The bobbing continues. By means of etiquette I still don't understand, his request is rejected. He returns to the horseshoe, ardour apparently (and, given his flies are open, measurably) undimmed.

"Often," Siobhan had conceded when I met her a few hours earlier in a pub, "the reality of a fantasy is more comedic. You do not always leave thinking, 'Oh my God, that was an amazing experience.' But it can be that too. The pleasure of it comes not from the building and the people you meet. It's about the change of dynamic and permission you give yourself by being there."

The rules of sex feel like they are changing. Not just sex in the reproduction sense, not even in the recreational sense. But in the gender sense, too. Here the only limitation to female promiscuity is the queue for the "lion cage" and the steady supply of condoms. Men can choose to watch, to participate, or to make a nice cup of tea in the kitchen.

"Like children, you play," said Siobhan. "Like kids who say, 'You be the astronaut, I'll be the doctor', you set the scenario and go – with agreed rules of engagement."

Men can even choose not to be men – at least in the conventional sense. "You get to be honest about what you want – who you are. You can dress up in stuff, maybe wear a leather skirt as a male because that's what you've always wanted to do, and can't in the office." There is at least one transgender participant, among the several hundred or more assembled.

What, in this steaming, heaving, suburban bungalow, do traditional ideas of gender and sex mean? And if the answer is, "very little", then why is the same not also true outside?

In the corner, on a sofa, there is an elderly couple: he dressed as if for the bridge game, she wearing an all-in-one see-through body-stocking. Later, come midnight, they will move next door, out of the cinema, for the food. Elsewhere, others will also stop what they are doing. They will leave behind the serried glory holes of the dungeon area (formerly a stables), the bubbles of the jacuzzi and the double bed of the exhibition room. They will congregate for the midnight meal: party food, naturally – with sandwiches cut into triangles.

Until the sandwiches arrive though, the elderly couple just watch.

In 2015, in Germany, a female student walked up to a stranger and repeated once again a phrase that has been repeated by psychology students since the 1970s. "I've noticed you around," she said. "I find you very attractive, would you go to bed with me?" As ever, the stranger said yes. This time, though, something was a little different.

It had been almost four decades since this experiment had first been performed, by Elaine Hatfield and Russ Clark. Their original investigation, described in the first chapter of this book, was not immediately recognised as the classic in the field that it became. For a long time, in fact, it was stuck in a drawer – unable to find a journal willing to publish it.

One journal rejected it saying, "If *Cosmopolitan* won't print it then *Penthouse Forum* might like it." Another said, only slightly more constructively, "This study is too weird, trivial and frivolous to be interesting. Who cares what the result is to such a silly question, posed in such a stranger-to-stranger way, in the middle of a Florida State University quadrangle? I mean, who cares other than *Redbook*, *Mademoiselle*, *Glamour* or *Self* – all of which would cream their jeans to get hold of this study?"

Andreas Baranowski, a researcher from Mainz University, was not so extreme in his criticism, but he did have concerns about the experiment. He just didn't think it felt right. He was prepared to believe women were not as keen as men on one-night stands, but zero per cent of them? "I have female friends who would tell me, sure I would have sex with a man if I really liked him. But not like that, not if he approached me in the street," he says.

What is it really measuring? Is it that women have a lower sex drive than men, or that they are more scared of going back to a stranger's apartment? Or just that, in recognition of the double standards that still exist in society, they have a "reputation" to think about?

So Dr Baranowski changed the parameters. First, he performed the experiment as it had been done before, on the streets – and got roughly the same results. Then he performed it in a more natural setting – a nightclub. Still the results were unchanged.[131] Finally, he created a situation where nobody would have to go back to anyone's apartment – where everyone was safe.

This required Baranowski to find an altogether more elaborate set up. He began by advertising for participants in a dating study. They were told they would be allowed to choose from a range of pictures of people who had also seen their photograph and wanted to have sex – and they could agree to meet with them in the safe environment of the university laboratory. It was a bit like a polaroid version of Tinder.

They were told the scientists would film the couple having a half-hour chat beforehand as part of an investigation into dating chemistry – then they and their potential lovers would be left to proceed. Obviously at every stage they could pull out, so to speak. "We couldn't force them to have sex," laments Dr Baranowski – university ethics boards are oddly stringent on threatening forced intercourse. But it was clear what the purpose of the meeting was. "They believed these people had already agreed to have sex with them. The point of this meeting was sex."

Of course, in reality, "it was a big cover story, just to get a few people in the lab."

It worked. He found that in this new context, men chose slightly over three women to meet for sex; women chose slightly under three. The difference between the two sexes in their urge for casual union seemed, superficially at least, to have narrowed considerably.

What does it mean? Some have interpreted the study as a total refutation of the original. Tom Stafford, a psychology lecturer at Sheffield University, wrote, "This new study gives an important update to an old research story which too many have interpreted as saying something about unalterable differences between men and women. The real moral may be about the importance of completely alterable differences in the way society treats men and women."

However, Baranowski, despite being warmly congratulated by Dr Stafford, does not see it as a refutation – more a revision. Neither does Professor Hatfield, the researcher who conducted the original experiment in the 1970s, who he said also sent him a note of congratulations. Which of them is right?

This book will offend people. Any book that looks at gender differences does, particularly if it explicitly accepts these differences exist. It is easy to see why. In a quote that most evolutionary scientists would rather forget, but feminists (and creationists) are determined they never will, Darwin said that man, thanks to sexual competition, "has ultimately become superior to woman".

"The chief distinction in the intellectual powers of the two sexes," he wrote in *The Descent of Man*, "is shewn by man attaining to a higher eminence, in whatever he takes up, than woman can attain – whether requiring deep thought, reason, or imagination, or merely the use of the senses and hands.

"If two lists were made of the most eminent men and women in poetry, painting, sculpture, music – comprising composition and performance, history, science, and philosophy, with half-a-dozen names under each subject, the two lists would not bear comparison. We may also infer, from the law of the deviation of averages, so well illustrated by Mr. Galton, in his work on 'Hereditary Genius', that if men are capable of decided eminence over women in many subjects, the average standard of mental power in man must be above that of woman."

Yikes. If in the past 40 years there has been a move among some academics to erase the idea of gender differences, and indeed gender itself, you can see why. If you let in a chink of a difference, even in somewhere apparently as far from intellect as sexual urges, how can you be certain the chink will not become a chasm in the dam holding back chauvinism?

In late 2017, James Damore, an employee at Google, made headlines across the world after writing an internal memo that questioned the company's diversity policies. He argued that it was not necessarily bias that kept women out of technology companies, but aptitude and interest. "We need to stop assuming that gender gaps imply sexism," he explained, before citing an array of research showing different preferences, abilities and attitudes between the sexes.

I have not spoken in this book about whether men are, say, innately better at computer science than women. I have, in fact, consciously avoided talking about any wider differences that do not closely relate to sex.

Partly, this is cowardice. Damore was sacked for his

thoughts. His internal document was condemned in newspapers, dinner parties and radio phone-ins around the world. As if that was not enough punishment, he was offered a job by Julian Assange.

Partly, it is because I genuinely don't know what to say about the relevance of such differences. I cannot deny that wider psychological differences can exist. In fact, it is scientifically dishonest to argue that some don't: it would be nothing short of a Darwinian miracle if males and females thought identically.* But knowing differences probably exist is different from saying what they are, and it is very different from saying they matter.

The further you get from sex, the less clear and more disputed the science of gender differences becomes. Cavemen definitely had sex; they definitely didn't programme computers. Can such psychological differences as may remain from those caveman days really ever explain major disparities in 21st-century employment?**

Partly, though, I decided to avoid talking about whether men are innately better at computer science because I distrust my impartiality. I am a man who studied computer science.

When I entered my fourth year of study at university, I was already used to a skewed gender ratio; my first degree was in maths. Anyone who tells you mathematicians are

---

* There are in fact consistent emotional differences found in men and women across cultures. Interestingly, some of them get larger, not smaller, in countries with greater gender equality.

** Sometimes the link between sex and modern aptitudes can be related to anatomy itself. In 2017 three researchers argued men do better at physics due to a more intuitive understanding of projectile motion – which they have because they are able to wee standing up. The study was not received without criticism.

unfairly stereotyped as geeky men has not been in a lecture at Cambridge's department of applied maths and theoretical physics on a warm summer's day.

As the sun heats the room, a gentle aroma rises from its occupants. Most of their T-shirts are black. Many display in-jokes of the "There are 10 kinds of people: those who understand binary and those who don't" variety. Most are the same T-shirts they wore the day before, and the day before that.

Yet even among us mathematics students, who long ago had accepted that a teenage interest in painting airfix models and programming graphical calculators doomed us to social obscurity, a hierarchy existed. At the top was the best mathematician at Trinity, itself the best mathematical college. Like a silverback gorilla, he taunted us with his virility from the front row, ostentatiously snogging the top female mathematician before pausing for breath to point out the lecturer's calculus mistakes. Between them, the couple had 16 As at A-level.

After taking that maths degree, I switched to computer science. Here, in one of my lecture courses, there was a woman we referred to as "Computer Science Girl". That was enough to distinguish her; there were no others.

I often think about Computer Science Girl, although for different reasons now than I did then. What was it like, turning up at those lectures every day? How did she cope with the isolation, the pathetic adoration – and most of all the implication that this was not the place for her gender?

Unlike James Damore, I cannot say whether women are on average worse or better at programming – the evidence is far from clear to me. I do know, though, that the effect of culture on this job is huge. I studied the subject in the early 2000s. Long before that, in the 1970s when the job lacked status, female programmers were in the majority.

What I can say is that one of the strongest conceivable ways of maintaining the current imbalance would be for future computer science girls to believe that it is not "natural" for them to study the subject.

But some gender differences do exist, and do matter. It matters that women get pregnant and men don't. It matters that women have a menopause and men don't. It matters that women can hide paternity. It matters that our hormones are different, that when we are promiscuous the way it manifests itself is different. It matters that even the way we are homosexual is different.

These forces can affect all our lives. After the James Damore scandal had died down, another took its place – involving Harvey Weinstein, the Hollywood producer. Numerous women accused him of abusing his position of power to sexually coerce them, or worse. Other professions tumbled – with revelations about the seedier side of the House of Commons, of academia, of journalism. Of anywhere, in fact, where men held status. Which was, of course, pretty much anywhere.

Was this about power dynamics? Of course. But was it also about sexual dynamics too? Surely.

Unless you can really imagine a scenario in which a post-menopausal female film mogul would – to take one accusation – entice young male actors to her hotel room then masturbate in front of them in a flowerpot, evolutionary forces matter. We can't change society without recognising what forces shaped that society in the first place.

Of course gender can be considered a continuum; it is

ridiculous to group all men and women together. Some men are more masculine than others, some like to crossdress. Some women are happy to be mothers and wives, some want to join the army and kill people. Some are gay, some are straight. But a continuum of behaviour between the sexes does not imply a uniform distribution of that behaviour. That genders overlap with each other does not mean that they are the same.

If that seems a facile point, I hope the research I have cited shows the implications are anything but. Sex isn't just sex. Sex is the reason we are here and the reason we evolve. It is our biological *raison d'être*, both in the sense that it is where we came from and in the sense that it dictates where we are going. It matters.

So yes, everything in human culture is changeable. We can build societies in which children are produced by harems of females, or ones such as the Ache in which males think they each have a bit share in a child. We can lock women up after puberty, mutilating their genitals to control their sexuality, or we can have cultures where it is the woman who decides who visits her each night – and where the fathers have no paternity rights at all.

The ability of humans to change their environment and culture is perhaps our defining attribute. Yet to understand how that works, in particular to understand the utter futility of separating nature and nurture, we also need to understand that changing the cultural norms does not necessarily mean changing the underlying rules.

How could changing norms and fixed rules explain the

results found by Dr Baranowski, and his latest iteration of the "Would you go to bed with me" experiment?

He initially wanted to see how much women's decisions to turn down the requests were a response to being afraid – and it seemed, by carefully tweaking the environment, they were. He also showed something else, though, something more surprising.

While the most striking finding of his study is that it shows women want more casual sex than we thought, it also seems – strangely – to imply men want a lot less. Given we know most men are willing to accede to any proposition on a street, why are they suddenly more choosy in this new context? Why didn't a majority of men in his experiment say yes to every proposition – rather than averaging at three of the ten?

Ever since the first student was propositioned in that Florida quadrangle in 1978, there has been a particular way of viewing the results of the "Would you go to bed with me" study.

The experiment, in this view, shows that men always want sex with strangers – and women always don't. But what is sometimes missed, or at least not fully appreciated, is that what those female experimenters were offering those hapless men was not just sex, it was no-strings sex.

In the real world men turn down offers from women every day, and one reason is that sex has consequences for them too. True, there is not a male version of pregnancy. But there is gossip, there is disapproval, there is what their friends think, there are expectations of relationships, there are marriage laws – there is child support. For women, biology imposes a high cost to sex while society – in the form of relationships and fathers – relieves some of that cost (while also reimposing the cost if they do it "wrong", by being promiscuous). In men it is precisely the reverse. Raw biology imposes no cost to sex; it is society that does that.

By enforcing half an hour of talking, Dr Baranowski's experiment added some of that society back in. In his laboratory what had in earlier experiments been no-strings sex had a few more strings – it was closer to a "normal" interaction.

That is not all that changed. The men in his experiment were also suddenly in the unusual position of having choice. In the original experiment, they would have said yes to every proposition – because they did not know if another would come. But here they could select from ten. So why not choose the three they liked best, and be sated with that?

"Since the men here could pick they could be more moderate. If you go to a place and I tell you you could pick any woman you want, you would choose carefully. For females it would be the same," says Dr Baranowski. "Only for females that's...kind of reality."

This is not about nature versus nurture. It is about nature *and* nurture. It is a feedback loop between the two.

"We are strong cultural beings – if you change the culture, biology will adapt. That's the awesome thing about the human brain. That does not mean genes are not a factor – just that they are very good at adapting a strategy that is good for them, in different environments."

So while the genes, and drivers, are innate, they are also adaptive to the situation. "It's about the economics of sex," says Dr Baranowski. "If men had a pact not to have sex with any female for ten years I'm sure we would have a gender-reversed society." Incredibly, a variety of that experiment has been tried – up to a point.

By the late 16th century, Sir Walter Raleigh was pretty sure he had located El Dorado. Piecing together scattered accounts from travellers and locals, he identified a site in the south-west of Guyana as the seat of the great fabled golden king. It was from here that one man reigned over a land of unimaginable wealth, a land which, wrote Raleigh, "for the greatness, for the riches, and for the excellent seat, it far exceedeth any of the world".

Raleigh, naturally, heard of all that wealth and decided to make it British.

Unfortunately for him, and Britain, all he found when he ventured deep into Guyana over the course of two expeditions was a vast savannah split by mountains – a land so poor, so unpromising for development, that it remains one of the world's great wildernesses. When he returned to Britain, having failed to fulfil his pledge to gain his monarch "a gold-rich empire more lucrative than Peru", he was beheaded for his efforts (and, admittedly, for killing a few too many Spaniards).

El Dorado may not exist, but in this land there live the Makushi, who have proved a source of metaphorical gold for anthropologists. To this day, many of the Makushi live in a way that would be recognisable to their ancestors. Subsistence farmers, they marry within the village, where they maintain the tradition of the husband-to-be proving himself by performing labour for his fiancée's family.

The modern world has reached even the Makushi. Increasingly, they are seeking their own El Dorado – leaving to build a more prosperous life in the surrounding regions.

The men go to become cattle ranchers and miners. The women leave to become maids and cleaners or work in shops in the cities.

Crucially, though, each village has made this change in different ways. In some, there has been a big exodus of women, in others both sexes have left in roughly equal numbers. In one, the largest, the men have gone and left the women behind.

In 2014 a team of anthropologists retraced the steps of Raleigh, and visited the Makushi. They went to the land described by Edgar Allan Poe in his poem "El Dorado" as "Over the Mountains of the Moon, Down the Valley of the Shadow", but more accurately described as lying in the south-western border region between Guyana and Brazil. They had come to look more closely at these varying sex ratios, and investigate whether the composition of the population changes promiscuity.

Using a standard "sociosexuality" questionnaire, the researchers explored the extent to which members of each community were prepared to engage in casual sex.[132]

They found that there was, for want of a better word, a market. When men were in abundance – when there was an oversupply of Y chromosomes – a traditionally female strategy prevailed. Men were as committed to monogamy as women. When men were in the minority, however, promiscuity was in the ascendant. Those who had gone to the mines or cattle ranches may have earned more money, but back home their brothers were still having a very profitable time.*

---

* Context can also affect what people do once they have reproduced – in quite grisly ways. In 19th-century Rajasthan, among the elite families daughters were not just rare, they didn't exist. They invested

When scientists used the same techniques to study attitudes to sex in 48 countries, they noted a similar trend. In the countries of Eastern Europe, where there had been high male suicide rates following the collapse of the USSR, women were more interested in short-term sex. Men were more in demand, so they got to dictate terms. Once again, humans adapt to the environment – nurture is hugely important. But the way they do so is dictated by nature.[133]

The same trade-off works at the level of individuals as well as nations. The most attractive men have more short term sexual partners, using their personal sexual capital to be promiscuous. The most attractive women have more long term partners – using their capital to shift the dating market to their more desired outcome.[134]

If this all sounds depressingly like a zero-sum game with the two sexes in opposition, there are tantalising hints that the two sexes could move closer to detente. The study of 48 countries found that in every country men were keener on no-strings sex. But it also found one factor that narrowed the gap irrespective of sex ratios – the proportion of women in parliament. In those countries with greater political, and presumably social, equality, women's views on sex were also likely to converge with men's. One potential explanation is that with economic freedom, reliance on males for economic

their efforts in sons, who could sire many children, and killed daughters at birth. So far, so depressingly patriarchal. In the lower castes, though, there was a reversal of the value attached to children. Sons could never compete with those higher up the social ladder but girls were valued not just as reproductive vessels, but as means of social betterment – of worth to those higher-caste sisterless boys. See Sarah Hrdy's *Mother Nature*, for an analysis of the ubiquity – and use – of infanticide.

support is less of a necessity – you don't have to worry about bagging a keeper.

Sometimes, context changes strategies for both sexes, in the same direction. Monogamy is useful in part because having a father around means the mother and baby get more resources. So it becomes less useful, under this theory, if there is an abundance of wealth. And indeed, if you show people slideshows of bling – fast cars, jewellery, mansions – and then test how much they want a long-term relationship, they seem to be less into one-night stands. If you show people instead pictures of potential dangers – spiders, snakes, cliff faces – then both sexes want more relationships of all types.[135] Live today; you could be dead tomorrow.

It's not that the rules have changed. It's that the situation has. Women still need to invest more in reproduction, men still gain benefit from every extra sexual encounter. Men are still, to a greater or lesser degree, Moulay Ismaels – yet the environment in which they construct their harem changes everything. Sexual power and sexual advantage shift. The same rules apply, but in a different context.

13

BACCHUS

The pursuit of pleasure

As in all parties, even swinger parties such as this one, the kitchen is the best place to be. Amid the chipped enamel mugs, the instant coffee and the laminate cupboards, everything feels comfortingly familiar. Elsewhere, nothing is familiar. Elsewhere, you never know when an erection will bob around a corner, like the gun of a Tiger tank appearing menacingly from behind a boulangerie in *Saving Private Ryan*.

It is almost midnight and things are hotting up. It turns out that even a night that begins with an orgy in a cinema can still hot up. A man peers into the kitchen with a big grin on his face. "Can I have a condom?" he asks. "Actually, two. I'm feeling lucky." A member of staff passes them over, and I head out to see where his luck will take him.

Siobhan, my guide to this world, had warned me it might all feel a bit alien at first. This is the "Greedy Girls" night – perhaps better termed "Hungry Boys" – where the main restriction on males is price. It is a £60 entrance fee for a single man, £10 for a single woman. Even this monetary difference does little to damp the male–female ratio.

Other swinger clubs have a policy always to actively limit men to those in couples, to make it less intimidating for women. Here, apart from the price weighting, they prefer to let people work out their own dynamic.

"There's an older couple in their seventies," says Siobhan. "They come, bring a picnic and are there all day. She gets to go off and play with all sorts of boys, and he has a little snooze. His libido has diminished as he got older, hers stayed the same. They've made it work." She says that couples often do make it work, provided they come with the right intentions.

For men not in a couple, though, the truth is, it is hard to make it work. When midnight arrives in the dungeon area, there is a minor scrum beside the "spider web". A woman has attached herself to the ropes, enmeshing her arms and legs in a cross like Leonardo da Vinci's *Vitruvian Man*.

Except a different image comes to mind. A black widow surrounded by her doomed harem, she is here seeking another mate. A dozen men jostle without wanting to appear to jostle, a great mass of elbows and shoulders trying to make it closer to the centre. One man is selected by the woman, another given a bit part. Beside me, on the periphery of the scrum, a man whispers dejectedly that the first man she chose is the one she came with, and that feels a little unfair. Slowly, the intensity of the jostling diminishes. Wordlessly, without coordination, the small pack of men moves to make a silent scrum elsewhere.

Men often have a misconception, when they come to these parties. "The single male is always charged a lot more money; that's just the way it is," says Siobhan. "However, that amount of money doesn't mean you're going to have sex that night, even if a lot think it does. No. The art of seduction is not dead in this particular world. It is very important to be good at chat, to be able to read people."

For single women, the dynamic is easier. Chat is not necessary. "They call us unicorns, because we are so rare. You're the person everybody wants to join them." That's why Siobhan has no intention of getting back with a boyfriend, preferring life as a lone wolf – and object of adulation. "If you walk through a door the men often try to go ahead of you, making a big performance of opening it for you. The ratio is doolally. They want to make contact in any way they can."

Most fail. "Some will just wander around all night. It's quite heartbreaking; it can be really soul-destroying as a single guy. But that's how it is."

The woman in the spider web has moved to the cage, the scrum following, looking for a second chance. Among them, I see the man who had asked for two condoms. He doesn't look so smiley any more. But that is how it works.

"It's the woman who decides," says Siobhan. "We get the final say. We always get the final say."

Here in this Home Counties bungalow, between the glory holes and the jacuzzi, the spider web and the cages, everything is completely different. And yet, it is not different at all.

Acknowledgements

The great privilege of my job is that I get to speak to intelligent women and men about their life's work. The great responsibility is that I then have to faithfully represent it. I am continually amazed at the willingness of scientists to give up their time, knowing if I get it wrong I imperil their reputation.

So I am indebted to the people who spoke to me, patiently answered stupid questions, and then in some cases also agreed to read and check the result. The book is better because of them – and any mistakes remain my own.

Most have their names in the text, but special thanks go to Qazi Rahman, who answered questions long after most reasonable people would have told me to go away; Joe Herbert, who proofread my testosterone chapter despite having a vastly more rigorous book of his own on the same subject; Gerulf Rieger, who tricked me into having my genital blood flow measured, and Oliver Moody, who read a chapter on false paternity while his wife was giving birth.

Then there were those who were not researchers but researchees. It is one thing to agree to have your sexuality studied for science, quite another to then talk to a journalist about it. Thanks in particular to Rosie Ablewhite, Sarah Nunn and Sam Schweiger. Thanks also to the Home Counties swingers, who welcomed me into their world.

This book would be a lot more boring without the team at Short Books, including Rebecca Nicolson, Paul Bougourd, Becke Parker and Evie Dunne. In particular, I would like to thank my editor Aurea Carpenter, who worked to cut back on the tediousness, expand the rest – and still respect the science.

I am grateful to Sarah Williams for excellent agenting, and *The Times* – who give me a wonderful job, time off to write about other things, and whose backing ensures in turn that other people take me seriously.

Finally, I would like to thank my family. My mother has not only had to put up with the combined trauma of a son and daughter-in-law writing about sex and religion respectively, but has even provided the childcare to facilitate it. My father has put up curtains, fences, blinds – and also spotted some fairly egregious nautical bloopers. Catherine has, as ever, supported me throughout.

I cannot honestly thank the boys for their help. The pram in the hall doesn't end it all, but it certainly slows things down. My revenge is that they will have to spend their teenage years knowing everyone read about their father's attendance at an orgy. Sorry.

References

1   Gates, G. 2011. How many people are lesbian, gay, bisexual, and transgender? *The Williams Institute.*

2   Clark, R. D. III & Hatfield, E. 2003. Love in the afternoon. *Psychological Inquiry.*

3   Clark, R. D. III & Hatfield, E. 1989. Gender differences in receptivity to sexual offers. *Journal of Psychology & Human Sexuality.*

4   McClintock, E. A. 2011. Handsome wants as handsome does: Physical attractiveness and gender differences in revealed sexual preferences. *Biodemography and Social Biology.*

5   Schmitt, D. P. 2005. Sociosexuality from Argentina to Zimbabwe: A 48-nation study of sex, culture, and strategies of human mating. *Behavioral and Brain Sciences.*

6   Bergström-Walan, M.-B. & Nielsen, H. H. 1990. Sexual expression among 60–80-year-old men and women: A sample from Stockholm, Sweden. *Journal of Sex Research*;

Johannes, C. B. & Avis, N. E. 1997. Gender differences in sexual activity among mid-aged adults in Massachusetts. *Maturitas*;

Ard, B. N. 1977. Sex in lasting marriages: A longitudinal study. *Journal of Sex Research*;

Julien, D. et al. 1992. Insiders' views of marital sex: A dyadic analysis. *Journal of Sex Research.*

7   Schmitt, D. P. et al. 2001. The desire for sexual variety as a key to understanding basic human mating strategies. *Personal Relationships.*

8   Bell, A. P. & Weinberg, M. S. 1978. *Homosexualities: A study of diversity among men and women.* New York: Simon & Schuster.

9   Baumeister, R. et al. 2001. Is there a gender difference in strength of sex drive? Theoretical views, conceptual distinctions, and a review of relevant evidence. *Personality and Social Psychology Review.*

10   Sheutz, M. & Arnold, T. 2016. Are we ready for Sex Robots? The Eleventh ACM/IEEE International Conference on Human Robot Interaction.

11   Weitbrecht, E. M. & Whitton, S. W. 2007. Expected, ideal,

and actual relational outcomes of emerging adults' "hook ups". *Personal Relationships.*

12   Murphy, S. 1992. *A Delicate Dance: Sexuality, celibacy, and relationships among Catholic clergy and religious.* New York: Crossroad.

13   Li, N. et al. 2011. Sexual conflict in mating strategies. *The Oxford Handbook of Sexual Conflict in Humans.*

14   González-Alvarez, J. & Cervera-Crespo, T. 2018. Gender differences in sexual attraction and moral judgment: research with artificial face models. *Psychological Reports.*

15   Mattle, B. & Wilson, A. 2009. Body size preferences in the potbellied seahorse Hippocampus abdominalis: choosy males and indiscriminate females. *Behavioral Ecology and Sociobiology.*

16   Galperin, A. et al. 2013. Sexual regret: Evidence for evolved sex differences. *Archives of Sexual Behavior;*

Morrison, M. et al. 2012. Life regrets and the need to belong. *Social Psychological and Personality Science.*

17   From Jones, W. 2016. *The Sex Lives of English Women: Intimate questions and unexpected answers.* London: Serpent's Tail.

18   Gallup G. G. Jr. et al. 2003. The human penis as a semen displacement device. *Evolution and Human Behavior.*

19   Huffard, C. L. et al. 2008. Mating behavior of *Abdopus aculeatus* (d'Orbigny 1834) (Cephalopoda: Octopodidae) in the wild. *Marine Biology.*

20   Koprowski, J. 1992. Removal of copulatory plugs by female tree squirrels. *Journal of Mammalogy.*

21   BBC. 2003. Penis is a competitive beast. *BBC News.* <http://news.bbc.co.uk/1/hi/health/3128753.stm>

22   Greiling, H. & Buss, D. 2000. Women's sexual strategies: The hidden dimension of extrapair mating. *Personality and Individual Differences.*

23   Scelza, B. A. 2013. Choosy but not chaste: Multiple mating in human females. *Evolutionary Anthropology.*

24   Cai, H. 2001. *A Society Without Fathers or Husbands: The Na of China.* New York: Zone Books.

25   Overy, C. et al eds. 2011. History of the National Survey of Sexual Attitudes and Lifestyles. *Wellcome Witnesses to Twentieth Century Medicine.* London: Queen Mary, University of London.

26 Pomeroy, W. B. 1972. *Dr Kinsey and the Institute for Sex Research*. New Haven: Yale University Press.

27 Beetz, A. & Podberscek, A. 2005. *Bestiality and Zoophilia: Sexual Relations with Animals*. London: Bloomsbury.

28 Alexander, M. G. & Fisher, T. D. 2003. Truth and consequences: Using the bogus pipeline to examine sex differences in self-reported sexuality. *Journal of Sex Research*.

29 Frederick, D. A. & Haselton, M. G. 2007. Why is muscularity sexy? Tests of the fitness indicator hypothesis. *Personality and Social Psychology Bulletin*;

Braun, M. & Bryan, A. 2006. Female waist-to-hip and male waist-to-shoulder ratios as determinants of romantic partner desirability. *Journal of Social and Personal Relationships*.

30 Kenrick, D. T. et al. 1993. Integrating evolutionary and social exchange perspectives on relationship: Effects of gender, self-appraisal, and involvement level on mate selection criteria. *Journal of Personality and Social Psychology*;

Kenrick, D. T. et al. 1990. Evolution, traits, and the stages of human courtship: Qualifying the parental investment model. *Journal of Personality*;

Regan, P. C. 1998. What if you can't get what you want? Willingness to compromise ideal mate selection standards as a function of sex, mate value, and relationship context. *Personality and Social Psychology Bulletin*.

31 Escasa, M. J. et al. 2011. Salivary testosterone levels in men at a US sex club. *Archives of Sexual Behavior*;

Roney, J. R. et al. 2009. Androgen receptor gene sequence and basal cortisol concentrations predict men's hormonal responses to potential mates. *Proceedings of the Royal Society B*.

32 Mazur, I. & Michalek, J. 1998. Marriage, divorce, and male testosterone. *Social Forces*;

Gettler, L. et al. 2011. Longitudinal evidence that fatherhood decreases testosterone in human males. *Proceedings of the National Academy of Sciences*.

33 Giotakos, O. et al. 2003. Aggression, impulsivity, plasma sex hormones, and biogenic amine turnover in a forensic population of rapists. *Journal of Sex and Marital Therapy*.

34   Fink, B. et al. 2007. A preliminary investigation of the associations between digit ratio and women's perception of men's dance. *Personality and Individual Differences.*

35   Stanton, S. J. et al. 2009. Dominance, politics, and physiology: voters' testosterone changes on the night of the 2008 United States presidential election. *PLoS One.*

36   Hines, M., 2007. Gender development and the human brain. *Annual Review of Neuroscience.*

37   Van Basten, J.P. et al. 1996. Fantasies and facts of the testes. *British Journal of Urology.*

38   Van Basten, J. P. et al. 1996. Fantasies and facts of the testes. *British Journal of Urology.*

39   Birmingham, S. 1982. *The Grandes Dames.* Guilford: Globe Pequot Press.

40   Anderson J. L. et al. 2016. Impact of testosterone replacement therapy on myocardial infarction, stroke, and death in men with low testosterone concentrations in an integrated health care system. *American Journal of Cardiology.*

41   Booth, A. & Osgood, W. 1993. The influence of testosterone on deviance in adulthood: assessing and explaining the relationship. *Criminology.*

42   Gimbel, C. & Booth, A. 1996. Who fought in Vietnam? *Social Forces.*

43   Johnston V. S. et al. 2001. Male facial attractiveness: evidence for a hormone-mediated adaptive design. *Evolution and Human Behavior.*

44   Booth, A. & Dabbs, J. 1993. Testosterone and men's marriages. *Social Forces.*

45   Fleming A. S. et al. 2002. Testosterone and prolactin are associated with emotional responses to infant cries in new fathers. *Hormones and Behavior.*

46   Lincoln, G. A. et al. 1972. The way in which testosterone controls the social and sexual behavior of the red deer stag (Cervus elaphus). *Hormones and Behavior.*

47   Klinesmith, J. et al. 2006. Guns, testosterone, and aggression: an experimental test of a mediational hypothesis. *Psychological Science.*

48   Dreher, J. et al. 2016. Testosterone causes both prosocial and anti-social status-enhancing behaviors in human males. *Proceedings of the National Academy of Sciences.*

49   Rowe, R. et al. 2004. Testosterone, antisocial behavior, and social dominance in boys: Pubertal development and biosocial interaction. *Biological Psychiatry.*

50   Perls, T. & Fretts, R. 1998. Why women live longer than men. *Scientific American.*

51   Canner, J. et al. 2014. US emergency department visits for fireworks injuries, 2006–2010. *Journal of Surgical Research.*

52   Headway, brain injury charity.

53   Kruger, D. & Nesse, R. 2006. An evolutionary life-history framework for understanding sex differences in human mortality rates. *Human Nature.*

54   Coates, J. M. & Herbert, J. 2007. Endogenous steroids and financial risk taking on a London trading floor. *Proceedings of the National Academy of Sciences.*

55   US Federal Bureau of Prisons.

56   Janicke, T. et al. 2016. Darwinian sex roles confirmed across the animal kingdom. *Science Advances.*

57   Brown, G. R. et al. 2009. Bateman's principles and human sex roles. *Trends in Ecology and Evolution;*

Jokela, M. et al. 2010. Serial monogamy increases reproductive success in men but not in women. *Behavioral Ecology.*

58   Karmin, M. et al. 2015. A recent bottleneck of Y chromosome diversity coincides with a global change in culture. *Genome Research.*

59   England, P. & McClintock, E. A. 2009. The gendered double standard of aging in US marriage markets. *Population and Development Review.*

60   Pollet, T. V. et al. 2013. The golden years: Men from the Forbes 400 have much younger wives when remarrying than the general US population. *Letters on Evolutionary Behavioral Science.*

61   Lanzenberger, R. et al. 2016. Testosterone affects language areas of the adult human brain. *Human Brain Mapping.*

62   Lieberman, D. et al. 2011. Kin affiliation across the ovulatory cycle: Females avoid fathers when fertile. *Psychological Science.*

63   Haselton, M. G. et al. 2007. Ovulatory shifts in human female ornamentation: Near ovulation, women dress to impress. *Hormones and Behavior*;

Haselton, M. & Gangestad, S. 2006. Conditional expression of women's desires and men's mate guarding across the ovulatory cycle. *Hormones and Behavior*;

Arslan, R. C. et al. 2017. Ovulatory changes in sexuality. *PsyArxiv*.

64   Garver-Apgar C. E. et al. 2007. Women's perceptions of men's sexual coerciveness change across the menstrual cycle. *Acta Psychologica Sinica*.

65   Krems, J. A. et al. 2016. Women selectively guard their (desirable) mates from ovulating women. *Journal of Personality and Social Psychology*.

66   Miller, S. & Maner, J. 2010. Scent of a woman: Men's testosterone responses to olfactory ovulation cues. *Psychological Science*.

67   Miller, G. et al. 2007. Ovulatory cycle effects on tip earnings by lap dancers: economic evidence for human estrus? *Evolution & Human Behavior*.

68   Lucassen, A. & Parker, M. 2001. Revealing false paternity: some ethical considerations. *The Lancet*.

69   Wang, G et al. 2017. Different impacts of resources on opposite sex ratings of physical attractiveness by males and females. *Evolution and Human Behavior*.

70   Durante, K. M. et al. 2012. Ovulation leads women to perceive sexy cads as good dads. *Journal of Personality and Social Psychology*.

71   Cousins, A. J. et al. 2015. Resistance to mate guarding scale in women: Psychometric properties. *Evolutionary Psychology*.

72   Moore, J. A. 1990. *Science as a Way of Knowing: The Foundations of Modern Biology*. Cambridge, MA: Harvard University Press.

73   Gilding, M. 2005. Rampant misattributed paternity: the creation of an urban myth. *People and Place*.

74   Bellis M.A. et al. 2005. Measuring paternal discrepancy and its public health consequences. *Journal of Epidemiology & Community Health*;

Larmuseau, M. H. et al. 2016. Cuckolded fathers rare in human populations. *Trends in Ecology and Evolution*.

Neel, J. V. & Weiss, K. M. 1975. The genetic structure of a tribal population, the Yanomama Indians. XII. Biodemographic studies. *American Journal of Physical Anthropology*.

Scelza, B. A. 2011. Female choice and extra-pair paternity in a traditional human population. *Biology Letters*.

75   Andersona, K. G. et al. 2007. Confidence of paternity, divorce, and investment in children by Albuquerque men. *Evolution and Human Behavior*.

76   Goetz, A. & Causey, K. 2009. Sex differences in perceptions of infidelity: Men often assume the worst. *Evolutionary Psychology*.

77   Maner, J. K. et al. 2008. Selective attention to signs of success: social dominance and early stage interpersonal perception. *Personality and Social Psychology Bulletin*.

78   Becker, D. V. et al. 2005. Concentrating on beauty: Sexual selection and sociospatial memory. *Personality and Social Psychology Bulletin*.

79   Oberzaucher E. & Grammer, K. 2014. The case of Moulay Ismael – Fact or fancy? *PLoS ONE*.

80   PlentyOfFish. 2014. Cited in: Metro.us. 2014. Online dating study describes "ideal" man and woman. *Metro*. <http://www.metro.us/lifestyle/online-dating-study-describes-ideal-man-and-woman/tmWnal---93jBoRJWtxsR2/>

81   OKCupid. 2015. Cited in: Xhou, L. 2015. Women on OKCupid don't seem to think their jobs are much of a selling point. *The Atlantic*. <http://www.theatlantic.com/business/archive/2015/09/men-women-market-themselves-okcupid/407671>

82   Toma, C. & Hancock, J. 2010. Looks and lies: The role of physical attractiveness in online dating self-presentation and deception. *Communication Research*.

83   Whitty, M. T. & Buchanan, T. 2010. What's in a screen name? Attractiveness of different types of screen names used by online daters. *International Journal of Internet Science*;

Khan, K. S. & Chaudhry, S. 2015. An evidence-based approach to an ancient pursuit: systematic review on converting online contact into a first date. *Evidence-Based Medicine*.

84   Bruch, E. et al. 2016. Extracting multistage screening rules from online dating activity data. *Proceedings of the National Academy of Sciences*.

85   Antfolk, J. 2018. Men's and women's youngest and oldest considered and actual sex partners. *PsyArXiv.*

86   Tyson, G. et al. 2016. A first look at user activity on Tinder. *ArXiv.*

87   Newitz, A. 2015. Ashley Madison code shows more women, and more bots. *Gizmodo.*

88   Långström, N. et al. 2010. Genetic and environmental effects on same-sex sexual behavior: A population study of twins in Sweden. *Archives of Sexual Behavior.*

89   Naz Project. 2011.

90   Vasey, P. & VanderLaan, D. P. 2014. Evolving research on the evolution of male androphilia. *Canadian Journal of Human Sexuality.*

91   Blanchard, R. 2017. Fraternal birth order, family size, and male homosexuality: Meta-analysis of studies spanning 25 years. *Archives of Sexual Behavior.*

92   Blanchard, R. et al. 2018. Male homosexuality and maternal immune responsivity to the Y-linked protein NLGN4Y. *Proceedings of the National Academy of Sciences.*

93   VanderLaan D. P. et al. 2012. Offspring production among the extended relatives of Samoan men and Fa'afafine. *PLoS ONE.*

94   Humphreys, L. 1970. *Tearoom Trade: Impersonal Sex in Public Places.* New Jersey: Aldine Publishers.

95   Power, R. 2015. Polygenic risk scores for schizophrenia and bipolar disorder predict creativity. *Nature Neuroscience.*

96   Chivers, M. L. et al. 2004. A sex difference in the specificity of sexual arousal. *Psychological Science.*

97   Diamond, L. 2009. *Sexual Fluidity: Understanding women's love and desire.* Cambridge, MA: Harvard University Press.

98   The National Survey of Sexual Attitudes and Lifestyles. 2012. *Natsal-3.*

99   Chivers, M. et al. 2007. Gender and sexual orientation differences in sexual response to sexual activities versus gender of actors in sexual film. *Journal of Personality and Social Psychology.*

100   Kennair, L. E. O. et al. 2015. Sex and mating strategy impact the 13 basic reasons for having sex. *Evolutionary Psychological Science.*

101   Holstege, G. 2005. European Society for Human Reproduction and Development conference.

102   Personal correspondence.

103   Hawkes K. et al. 1989. Hardworking Hadza grandmothers. In Standen, V. eds. 1989. *Comparative Socioecology: The behavioural ecology of humans and other mammals.* Oxford: Blackwell Scientific Publications.

104   Voland, E. & Beise, J. 2001. Opposite effects of maternal and paternal grandmothers on infant survival in historical Krummhörn. *Behavioral Ecology and Sociobiology.*

        Gemmill, A. & Catalano, R. 2017. Do post-reproductive aged females promote maternal health? Preliminary evidence from historical populations. *Evolution, Medicine, and Public Health.*

105   Department of Health and Human Services. 2014

106   Julka, C. 1999. Viagra as Pandora's box for the elderly. *Elder Law Journal.*

107   Otto, S. 2008. Sexual reproduction and the evolution of sex. *Nature Education.*

108   Parker, G. A. et al. 1972. The origin and evolution of gamete dimorphism and the male-female phenomenon. *Journal of Theoretical Biology.*

109   Rowson, E. 1991. The effeminates of early Medina. *Journal of the American Oriental Society.*

110   Augustine. *City of God.*

111   Stryker, S. & Whittle, S. 2006. *The Transgender Studies Reader.* London: Routledge.

112   Drescher, J. & Pula, J. 2014. Ethical issues raised by the treatment of gender-variant prepubescent children. *The Hastings Center Report.*

113   Allen, L. S. & Gorski, R.A. 1990. Sex difference in the bed nucleus of the stria terminalis of the human brain. *Journal of Comparative Neurology.*

114   Smitha, E. S. et al. 2015. The transsexual brain – a review of findings on the neural basis of transsexualism. *Neuroscience & Biobehavioral Reviews.*

115   BMJ Best Practice Monograph. 2015.

116   Blanchard, R. 1993. Varieties of autogynephilia and their relationship to gender dysphoria. *Archives of Sexual Behavior.*

117   Nuttbrock L. et al. 2011. A further assessment of Blanchard's typology of homosexual versus non-homosexual or autogynephilic gender dysphoria. *Archives of Sexual Behavior.*

118   Lawrence, A. 2004. Autogynephilia: A paraphilic model of gender identity disorder. *Journal of Gay and Lesbian Psychotherapy.*

119   *Ethnographic Atlas Codebook.*

120   Surbech, M. et al. 2017. Male reproductive skew is higher in bonobos than chimpanzees. *Current Biology.*

121   Muller, M. N. et al. 2006. Male chimpanzees prefer mating with old females. *Current Biology.*

122   Henrich, J. et al. 2012. The puzzle of monogamous marriage. *Philosophical Transactions of the Royal Society B.*

123   Daoulah, A. et al. 2017. Polygamy and risk of coronary artery disease in men undergoing angiography: An observational study. *International Journal of Vascular Medicine.*

124   Strassmann, B. 1997. Polygyny as a risk factor for child mortality among the Dogon. *Current Anthropology.*

125   Gibson, K. 2009. Differential parental investment in families with both adopted and genetic children. *Evolution and Human Behavior.*

126   Jankowiak, W. et al. 2005. Co-wife conflict and cooperation. *Ethnology.*

127   Geary, D. et al. 2014. Reflections on the evolution of human sex differences: Social selection and the evolution of competition among women. *Evolutionary Perspectives on Human Sexual Psychology and Behavior.*

128   Leenaars, L. S. et al. 2008. Evolutionary perspective on indirect victimization in adolescence: the role of attractiveness, dating and sexual behavior. *Aggressive Behavior.*

129   Davis, A. C. et al. 2017. Gossip as an intrasexual competition strategy: Sex differences in gossip frequency, content, and attitudes. *Evolutionary Psychological Science.*

130   Henrich, J. et al. 2012. The puzzle of monogamous marriage. *Philosophical Transactions of the Royal Society B.*

131   Baranowski, A. & Hecht, H. 2015. Gender differences and

similarities in receptivity to sexual invitations: Effects of location and risk perception. *Archives of Sexual Behavior.*

132   Schacht, R. & Mulder, M. B. 2015. Sex ratio effects on reproductive strategies in humans. *Royal Society Open Science.*

133   Schmitt, D. P. 2005. Sociosexuality from Argentina to Zimbabwe: A 48-nation study of sex, culture, and strategies of human mating. *Behavioral and Brain Sciences.*

134   Rhodes, G. et al. 2005. Attractiveness and sexual behavior: Does attractiveness enhance mating success? *Evolution and Human Behavior.*

135   Thomas, A. G. & Stewart-Williams, S. 2018. Mating strategy flexibility in the laboratory: Preferences for long- and short-term mating change in response to evolutionarily relevant variables. *Evolution and Human Behavior.*

Index

Tom Whipple is the award-winning science editor of the London *Times*. This is his second book. *How to Win Games and Beat People* was published by Random House in the UK and HarperCollins in the US in 2015.